AT ROAD'S END

*Robert Lee's Extraordinary
Journey to Forgiving a
Heinous Murder*

DAVID WAYNE BROWN

Epigraphs
With Robert Lee

SARTORIS
LITERARY
GROUP

SARTORIS LITERARY GROUP
Metro-Jackson, Mississippi
www.sartorisliterary.com

Dedication

*This book is for Ann and the children,
Dorene, Bobby, and Elizabeth (Liz).*

Mary Walton —
thanks from us both.

[signature]

To Mary Walton
a good friend indeed

[signature]

Acknowledgements

I wish to thank the Fayette County Sheriff's Department, particularly Det. Don W. "Chuck" Pugh (deceased), and Det. Ricky Wilson; Fayette County Assistant Attorney Gen. Colin Campbell; the Collierville Police Department, especially Det. Lt. Tom Beard, retired, Det. S.A. Young, Det. Lloyd Shelton (retired and living in Florida), and Det. Lt. Gannon Hill; Agent C.M. Sturgis, with the FBI; Tony R. Arvin, Asst. U.S. Attorney, and his wife Maureen; the Germantown Police Department; the Shelby County Victim Assistance Center and Susan Gillpatrick, and the staff at Hollywood Casino in Tupelo, Mississippi.

And thanks to my wife Mary for her unwavering support, and scores of people who gave me comfort in my hour of need.

— Robert Lee

Many thanks to Deborah M. Clubb for her judicious editing and suggestions, Jim Dickerson for encouragement, and Bob Lee for sharing his story in the hope of helping others.

— David Wayne Brown

Cover art is by Madison Lee, granddaughter of Ann and Bob Lee

CONTENTS

FOREWORD

At Road's End chronicles one family's journey of forgiveness. All of us have experienced slights of one kind or another; that's just part of the human experience. But few of us have been forced to navigate the horrific events experienced by the Lee family in the summer of 1999 which continue to impact their lives. As Bishop of the Episcopal Diocese in West Tennessee since 2019, it has been my privilege to share a small portion of this journey with Bob Lee.

Forgiveness is a central tenant of Christianity. The New Testament includes two versions of the Lord's Prayer, Jesus's recommendation for one way to approach God in prayer. The longer version of the Lord's Prayer is part of the Sermon on the Mount in the Gospel of Matthew (*Matthew 6:9-13*), whereas a shorter version is found in Luke's Gospel (*Luke 11:2-4*). In both versions, the faithful are asked to forgive others because of the forgiveness they have received from God. Our forgiveness springs forth out of appreciation for everything God has done for us through Jesus Christ. Whenever we pray the Lord's Prayer, we simultaneously ask our Father for forgiveness and recommit to the spiritual practice of forgiveness in our own lives.

Jesus includes a longer discussion about forgiveness in *Matthew 18*, prompted by a question from the disciple Peter. Peter asks how often he should forgive someone who sins against him. He wonders aloud if seven times would be sufficient. That may sound generous to us, but as is so often the case, Jesus's perspective transcends our understanding. Jesus instructs Peter not to stop forgiving after the seventh offense but to continue forgiving 77 times. And the number 77 is not meant to be taken literally. We are not absolved from the responsibility of forgiving after the 78th offense. Jesus uses a large number to suggest that our capacity to forgive should be infinite.

Why might it be so important to God that we demonstrate forgiveness? Quite simply, the quality of our lives depends in part upon our capacity for forgiveness. This isn't primarily about the person who harmed us. Forgiveness is about us. It is the key to releasing our anger and frustration from the wounds inflicted by others. Let me be clear: forgiveness is not synonymous with forgetting. Our memories are an essential aspect of what it means to be human, and we are not called to discard or repress the painful events in life. In fact, it's impossible to forget the past. But without processing these events, we can become stuck.

So let us acknowledge that forgiveness is a spiritual practice. It's a way of life, not a one time event, and requires intentionality on our part. Consider your prayer life. You don't pray once then decide I don't need to pray anymore. We continue to pray because it is one of the ways we maintain our connection with God. Prayer is a lifelong process, and so is forgiveness. And like any other spiritual muscle, the more we practice forgiveness the better we become.

Part of the process may involve reaching out to those who have harmed us, although this isn't appropriate in every situation. Even if we reach out, the offender may not be open to communication. Regrettably, some offenders never express remorse for their actions. Or the offender may be deceased. Regardless of whether we have the ability to confront the person who hurt us, we can work through our issues so that we move on with our lives.

Therefore, a community of support is an important aspect of forgiveness. Sharing our stories and receiving feedback from others are key steps in the process. Family members, trusted friends, clergy persons, therapists and spiritual directors can all be of assistance on this journey. I have encountered many people who were willing to offer their support when I was in the midst of a difficult situation. We may be reluctant to acknowledge we need assistance, but you may be surprised by the resources at your disposal when you reach out for help. None of us are meant to go through life on our own, and there's no shame in admitting that some situations are beyond our capacity to handle alone.

Another aspect of forgiveness is that healing involves pain. Physical healing and psychological healing include periods of discomfort. After surgery, you don't immediately return to your regular routine. It takes time to rebuild your physical stamina and the same is true when we have been psychologically or emotionally wounded. Bob and his family have acknowledged how difficult this process has been, and it's still painful. Yet there's freedom on the other side of healing. Laying down our burdens enables us to move into the future with hopefulness and purpose.

The good news is that the Lord doesn't just encourage forgiveness. God also facilitates forgiveness. In our 21st century society, keeping score seems to be the name of the game. We are quick to hold onto grievances large and small, and to retain our anger for years. Left to our own devices, we don't have the capacity in and of ourselves to forgive. God alone can heal the brokenness in our lives. The only way we can survive the difficult seasons of life is to put all of our faith, hope and trust in the Lord. When we turn to God and ask God to facilitate forgiveness in our lives, amazing things can happen. God works in mysterious ways and the process can take years, but many of us wake up one morning and the burning anger we felt toward our offender is gone. We don't understand how or why, but thanks be to God for the grace of forgiveness. Come Holy Spirit, come and reveal the new life available to us when we forgive.

The Rt. Rev. Phoebe A. Roaf

Bishop, Episcopal Diocese of West Tennessee
The Day of Pentecost: Whitsunday
May 23, 2021

PROLOGUE

Until he heard the sound of tires on dirt and gravel, Otis had hardly moved for more than an hour.

After freeing himself from the old section of barbed wire, he had crossed quickly to the shallow ditch, to where he knew he was supposed to be. And there he stayed, his head on his front paws, waiting. Late afternoon shade drifted toward the east side of the narrow strip of woods.

Now he sat up, fully alert, as cars came into view.

The officers who got out were kind. Even so, he scampered away several yards before timidly walking toward them.

"It's okay, boy. C'mon."

Their tone seemed trustworthy.

Near the side of the road Otis looked searchingly at the pile of rugs, sticks and tree limbs that covered the temporary resting place of what had been the center of his life and his loyalty. Then he climbed into the back of one of the vehicles.

Perhaps these men in uniforms would make things right.

One stood looking down where Otis had been, preparing himself for what he was about to see, as a second went looking for the .22 rifle. A third man pointed at the leash. "Look," he said. "They had him tied to that old fence. He must've struggled quite a while to get out of that collar."

Barbara Ann Lee and her constant companion Otis take
a break from horse training duties at New Venture Farm.

ONE

I awake early before the alarm sounds. Today is going to be a busy one. I slept lightly overnight, anticipating our trip to Albuquerque, New Mexico. We are heading west to go camping in the Jemez Mountains with our daughter Liz.

Everything is planned in detail. We have shopped for gear and uncovered some camping items we were given for Christmas. I have some last-minute stuff to do this morning at work. The barely-used '97 Chevy Blazer Ann bought a week and a half ago is ready. We test-packed it yesterday. Otis kept slipping on the leather seats, so we bought some non-slip bathroom rugs for him to lie on.

I shower, make coffee, grab a couple of bagels for breakfast and leave some for Ann. She and Otis — "night people" — are no doubt still in bed.

I peek in the bedroom. Two sets of eyes are closed. I bend down and kiss Ann. "See you later, honey." Otis opens his eyes and puts up his head for a pat. "Take care of your Mom, Otis."

They were just words I said most mornings. They will mean so much to me later on.

As I drive the pickup the fifty miles to my computer network supervisor's job at the casino in Tunica, Mississippi, I feel my excitement mounting. We've never been much on taking vacations. This is going to be our first big one that doesn't involve horses.— **Robert Lee.**

* * *

How many ways can a dozen lives be lived in the normal, even mundane activities of a given day — how many directions and choices taken — before their paths come inexorably together forever? It's possible to trace the lines on one specific, tragic day in time, and in one place in the midsection of the United States of America: Collierville, Tennessee, Tuesday, June 15, 1999.

Those intersecting lines can't be altered later. Not a single step changed. Not one decision rescinded. Not in this wide world.

* * *

It's about 8:10 that summer morning. Eric Glover, 16 and big for his age, wakes up on the back seat of a car on South Street in Collierville, a town situated on the outskirts of Memphis at the eastern border of Shelby County, Tennessee. Less than a mile south of the town's limits is the Mississippi state line.

Down south from Chicago only a few months, the teenager sometimes has to spend the night in the old car because the house where his cousin's family lives has only three small rooms. Some nights quite a few people need a bed or couch. Last night was one. He yawns, stretches, and remembers vaguely he's supposed to help his cousin, 17-year-old Antonio Carpenter, get the car running again. Eric thinks about walking to the door and shouting

This house is where 12 members of the Carpenter family lived on Yager Road in rural Fayette County, Tennessee in 1999.

for Antonio to get up. Then he remembers another plan for the day: a nefarious and evil plan, if poorly constructed.

Under a nearly cloudless sky the temperature already is inching toward scorching territory. The month has been typically summery in the Mid-South region of the country — hot and uncomfortably humid. The forecast for today includes a zenith of 95 degrees Fahrenheit around 2 p.m. Rain is nowhere in sight. Only a few wispy clouds hover just above the horizon.

Eric Glover stretches again and realizes he's hungry. He'll have to talk Antonio into going for some food — if he ever wakes up. Or maybe Antonio's brother will be by soon in his car.

Nineteen miles east in neighboring Fayette County,

Antonio's brother is already up. In fact Robert Carpenter, Jr., a year older than "Tony" at nineteen, has pulled on some clothes and eased out of the four-room, low-lying house 750 feet off Yager Road. This house also holds wall-to-wall people. Robert has 13 siblings besides Antonio. Most of his younger brothers and sisters are in the house, still asleep. He climbs behind the steering wheel of his 1984 four-door, dusty blue Buick LeSabre with a tan top and points the hood toward Collierville.

A few houses from where Eric Glover is thinking about food, Jonathan Guy begins his morning walk two and a half blocks to the Sonic Drive-in where he has worked as a cook for a month. He's the quiet one in a circle of friends and acquaintances who work or hang out at the fast food restaurant. Two years from today he'll begin serving an eight-year sentence at a notorious Mississippi prison for two armed robberies. Today he's just a short-order cook looking forward to the next payday, not thinking beyond that.

At Sonic, Lamont Nunley, a.k.a. Mont Nunnally, also a resident of South Street, has already arrived for work. Self-assured and carrying his usual air of braggadocio, he is known to steal from his employer. When the managers aren't looking he sneaks free meals out a back door to friends and acquaintances, people like Eric Glover and the Carpenter brothers, whenever they pull into one of the car slots where orders are placed, or when they walk to the restaurant from a nearby parking lot. They all know each other, smoke joints together, and brag about drug deals. They talk about the gangs they claim they're in and the gangs' various colors and signs. All have been in trouble to one degree or another.

Mont likes to wear his gang's colors at work.

No one tells him he can't.

At 9 a.m. Joshua Smith is already working at the NAPA Auto Parts shop, next door to Sonic. Business is light and so is his workload. He heads out to the parking lot to work on his own car. Soon he will notice three men sitting in the LeSabre, "doing nothin', just sittin'."

The Buick leaves and drives slowly through the Sonic lot, then it returns to NAPA and parks in a different location.

Cruising the busy Collierville streets, meanwhile, Detective Scott Young, not for the first time, drives on U.S. Route 72 past NAPA and the Sonic, on the way into the center of town. Everything is peaceful, routine. Rush hour traffic filled with folks headed to Memphis for work is over. He may have to roll up his windows and turn on the AC today. Colleague Gannon Hill is in another patrol car across town, parked and watching for speeders. Their radio scanners mostly keep silent.

Just over the county line, Fayette County Sheriff's Office Investigator Don (Chuck) Pugh is about as bored as Young and Hill. Pugh's thinking he might run home for lunch with his girlfriend later today and informs the dispatcher of his plan. Pugh, coincidentally, lives on the same country road where the Carpenters live.

It is a minute or two after 9 when Barbara Ann Lee calls her husband Robert (Bob) Lee from their home in nearby Germantown, another Memphis suburb that lies snugly around the same federal Highway 72. The wide road is known locally as Poplar Avenue and runs eastward from the Mississippi River through the heart of Memphis, into Germantown, finally cutting through the center of Collierville. There U.S. 72 diverges from

State Highway 57. Poplar here follows 57 straight east, while the federal highway takes a southeast turn toward Mississippi and Alabama. The NAPA Auto store and Sonic Drive-in hug alongside U.S. 72 as it leaves (and enters) Collierville.

Ann confirms by phone what Bob already knows about her morning ahead: quick stops at the post office and the bank on the way to the horse barn in a rural part of Germantown. After she gives final instructions to her workers there she'll grab lunch at one of her usual stops in Collierville and then she'll go home to finish packing.

Ann manages a horse farm for local trainer Randy Mullins. She's worked at New Venture Farm for fifteen years, keeping the books, supervising barn workers James, Francisco, Sabino and Big Joe, acquiring feed supplies, generally keeping the stables smoothly running, and making sure the horses are fed, groomed, healthy. She's a hard-working, no nonsense but kind-hearted woman, curly blonde hair going to gray.

Ann also spends time teaching youngsters how to ride their horses and ponies in an adjacent corral here and other places around Collierville and Germantown. She is a beloved fixture in local horse circles. The equestrian industry is big in Shelby County. In fact, Shelby, which encompasses Memphis and six suburbs, is known for having more horses per capita than any other county in the nation.[i]

"Honey," she says now. "How much cash money do you want me to get at the bank?"

"A couple hundred should be enough. The rest we can put on plastic."

It was one of those quick conversations people have every

22

Ann and Otis visit with friends between equestrian events at the Germantown Charity Horse Show. Ann worked with horses all her life as a rider, trainer and breeder. She was a fixture at the Germantown, TN Charity Horse Show, one of the biggest multi-breed shows n the country, including hunters, jumpers, Arabians, American Saddlebred and Tennessee Walking horses. Riders compete from the age of five and older.

day. Nothing out of the ordinary. Just words spoken with a certain tone of expectation. Bob later would remember every word — no, every syllable — spoken that day between them. Of course, he would.

Ann strokes Otis, a three-year-old grey Standard Schnauzer, her constant companion. They leave the house and walk out to that green 1997 Blazer that will never make the drive to New Mexico. The have last-minute errands and chores to get done. She didn't tell Bob but she also plans to stop at the Eddie Bauer store to buy him shirts and jeans, a surprise for the trip.

Otis climbs eagerly into the back of the SUV and settles on the new rugs, satisfied, ready for the ride and a late lunch. He hates the pauses at the store and at the Germantown post office when Ann again leaves him in the car to go check her box. The First Tennessee Bank branch is another thing entirely. There he gets treats from the cashiers. This particular morning they are greeted at the drive-through window by a smiling Gwen Taylor. The clerk handles a deposit for the ranch, then a personal deposit with cash back. She passes ten 20-dollar bills to Ann. They exchange pleasantries.

Ann begins a sunny drive toward Collierville. It's time to grab a bite to eat.

For Bob, this fine morning is crawling by. For once he's not busy at the riverside casino. He's ready to get on the road and wonders if he's forgotten anything.

No, he tells himself. Ann's so organized. Everything is just fine.

TWO

I think back and realize we really didn't take very many actual vacations. Went on a short cruise once. Our lives were built around our work and raising our family — two daughters, Liz and Dorene, and a son, Robert Jr., or Bobby.

And horses, of course. Ann trains horses, teaches children all the riding techniques. Together we managed the West Tennessee Hunter Jumper Association, which puts on several horse shows throughout the year.

At night we usually watched TV. There was homework and work around the house. We were just a family, you know? Sometimes we worked seven days a week.

I don't know where those thirty-nine years of our marriage went.

* * *

Sheran Diane Bryson works as a carhop at Sonic. Tuesdays are one of her workdays. Today, customers are keeping her busy, coming and going in and out of the sun.

She recognizes frequent visitor Ann Lee drive up in the green Blazer with Otis. Ann, her dog and even the new car are known to several of the workers. After a few minutes the carhop strides from the restaurant with Ann's order of food on a tray, heading for parking slot 22. At this particular Sonic, servers don't use roller skates.

It is 1:29 p.m., investigators will judge later. Otis stands, ears up, his nearly tailless back end swaying. He likes the Sonic French fries, so he sometimes gets his own small order.

Slot 22 is on Sonic's south side, near the back of the restaurant's lot. Sheran walks out the side door but comes to a sudden stop when she sees a sight she will testify later she'll never forget: two young males where they shouldn't be. One is sitting in the back seat of Ann's car. The other is standing by the driver's side, holding what she describes later as a long black gun, and wearing a light blue windbreaker.

Frightened, she darts back into the restaurant, tells the manager what she just saw and ducks down on the floor, crying. The manager calls 9-1-1.

Jonathan Guy, the short-order cook, would recall the same scene inside the restaurant in a deposition taken two years later at the state prison in Parchman, Mississippi:

"After taking a short break, I returned inside the Sonic, went to the restroom, washed my hands and returned to my workstation. Suddenly, a carhop ran inside, started throwing things everywhere and yelling to call 9-1-1 because there were three men with guns and they were taking a woman in her car."

Two men? Three men? Guns, plural?

This won't be the only time the pertinent "facts" in what will be a lengthy murder case prosecuted in state and federal courts, plus a later civil lawsuit, will scatter widely like so many pellets from a shotgun blast.

Sheran's account, though, will prove to be the crucial eyewitness description of a tragic abduction — a carjacking that will end in a tortuous death on a rough farm road to nowhere in woods hugging a fallow field in nearby Fayette County, half a mile north of the Mississippi line.

The crime — nonsensical and horrendous in how it is carried out — will grab local headlines and TV news coverage for more than a year, will lead to jurisdictional disputes and will fiercely anger the people who knew Ann — and many who didn't know her. This will be a homicide case that made no sense and yet seemed destined to be carried out by a trio of unthinking and uncaring misfits, if that mild description can be justly used for the very bad young actors that day.

The murder will draw U.S. Attorney General Janet Reno's personal permission to be tried as a death penalty case in federal court. It will interrupt lives, and will leave unanswered nagging questions decades later.

The case also will send Ann's husband on a long dark night's flight of his soul as he tries to work through unfamiliar thoughts, pains and emotions. At times he won't even recognize himself.

* * *

One minute after the 9-1-1 call is answered, the Blazer's gone. As it pulls onto the highway a passerby spots the gun and makes the second call to 9-1-1, on a flip-top cell phone. Police cars head to Sonic. There Sheran Bryson says she didn't recognize the two men she saw. That will ring untrue a year later when she and others are deposed by attorneys.

A few streets away, Ann Lee is now sitting on the passenger side of the moving SUV, her shock and fear growing. The driver steers the Blazer with his left hand and holds a sawed-off rifle in his right. The muzzle is aimed at her head. She doesn't know the rifle is empty. Otis is frightened. He pants and whines in her lap.

Ann, trying to think, is unaware that she has less than an hour to live. She tries to stay calm. Repeatedly she attempts to talk her way free, all the while petting Otis and telling him everything is all right — so her carjackers would later tell police during interrogations.

"I need my medication," Ann says. "I'm a diabetic."

No response.

"And my dog is an epileptic. He needs his phenobarbital."

Someone laughs.

She pleads to be let out of the car.

"We can't let you go," the driver barks. "You'll turn us in."

"Of course I will. But if you let me go out here in the country it'll be a long time before I can even get to a phone."

All along the fourteen-mile drive into the next county, she keeps talking, outwardly calm, even as the three others in her vehicle bicker about what to do with her. They go through her purse and remove the cash from her wallet. Now armed robbery is added to aggravated kidnapping and the federal crime of carjacking. They make fun of the family photos they find and deride the country western music playing on the radio.

One can only imagine the growing terror Ann Lee felt in that half-hour ride to a dead-end farm road. Her killers later said she bargained for her life, and begged that her dog not be harmed. That won't surprise her family when they hear those words in court. She and Otis were an inseparable pair.

From the very first moment, this was a hijacking that lacked any kind of common sense or planning, even though the three took steps the night before to carry out just such a crime.

The big question, heavy in the silence of no answer, is Why? What was the purpose, other than mayhem and evil?

After leaving Sonic, the Blazer winds through an industrial part of Collierville and then turns toward Fayette County on U.S. 57. As it does, the Collierville police dispatcher sends a BOLO — Be On The Lookout — for two or three young black males and a white woman in a 1997 green Chevrolet Blazer. Officers for ten miles around are tuning in, Mississippi patrolmen included.

Carjackings and abductions rarely occur in this part of the county. Memphis maybe. But the quiet satellite town of Collierville?

At the Sonic, Detective Young arrives in his cruiser, screeching to a stop. He begins investigating the scene and is soon joined by Hill. The carhop explains again how she saw a tan-over-dark-blue car parked next to Ann's, one man in her back seat and a second man with a "long gun" standing at the driver's door of the Blazer.

Young soon locates an old Buick next door in the NAPA lot. There Joshua Smith gives a description of *three* men who had parked there twice that morning. At one point, around 1:15 p.m. or so, the driver got out of the car and asked to use the restroom, then came out and asked him how long he was going to work on his car. Smith thought that was odd. The Buick left.

Smith recounts that he went into the store for about five

minutes. When he returned outside, the Buick was back, parked in a different spot, empty. He tells Young he didn't notice anything happening at Sonic, though.

The detective gets on the radio. He soon traces ownership of the Buick. It is registered to a Robert Carpenter on Yager Road outside Moscow, Tennessee, a twenty-five-minute drive east in Fayette County.

As Young radios back and forth with the dispatcher, another Collierville police cruiser is flagged down by a frantic motorist. The witness reports seeing a Blazer driving eastbound on Poplar, now Route 57, not far from the Shelby-Fayette line. The driver, the citizen says, a black man, was holding a gun on a white woman in the passenger side of the car.

Now police radios are crackling overtime. Several voices — some excited, some more subdued — crowd the air.

At Don Pugh's home at 1065 Yager Road, three miles from the hamlet of Moscow, the phone rings. Pugh is a short fireplug of a man known to his friends as Chuck. Since he signed out for lunch his police radio is turned off. He takes another bite of his sandwich, then answers the phone to hear the excited voice of the Fayette County Sheriff's dispatcher. She tells him of the carjacking and the BOLO.

"They had a vehicle there at the NAPA next to Sonic that they thought possibly was involved in this carjacking and it was registered to Robert Carpenter at 4680 Yager," he later reports under oath. The address is only two miles up the road from his home.

"I went directly to the address and when I arrived there I spoke with three black males I presumed to be juveniles. There

30

were several children there, too." While questioning them he is joined by two other officers. They notice fresh tire tracks.

"Oh, that's from when our Daddy was here last night," the officers are told by one of the teens.

"At this time I was under the assumption that I was looking for Robert's daddy," Pugh said. "I know his daddy well ... they told me he was at work."

Pugh radios the dispatcher to get someone to call the Alpha Corporation, a polyester resin manufacturing plant in Collierville where Robert Carpenter was employed. Pugh soon learns that Carpenter is working at the plant as scheduled. Now the detective realizes he must be looking for the son, Robert Carpenter, Jr.

Pugh, remembering that Junior had been in some trouble before, questions the young people at the house further. They swear that they saw the younger Robert the night before in Collierville, but they haven't seen him this day. Pugh doesn't know they are point-blank lying to him.

Back in the cruiser Pugh hears a second BOLO — this time about the motorist who had spotted the driver of a green Blazer holding a gun on a woman passenger.

"At that point we realized we did have a vehicle coming into Fayette County," he testified. The three officers divide up territory.

"I proceeded to Moscow to check that area." While headed to the small town Pugh hears a broadcast identifying Ann Lee as having been kidnapped. The alert also gives the vehicle's make, model and tag number.

"In Moscow I checked out local hang-outs — the Perkins restaurant and stores that were open," he said. Seeing nothing suspicious and no sign of the Blazer, Pugh's instincts tell him to return to the Yager Road address to find a location where he can sit in his car and have a view of the dirt drive that leads to the house.

"I went south of the house approximately 300 yards to an old cemetery and pulled in. But I could only see where the driveway intersected Yager Road. That area's a flood land with a lot of straggly bushes. It's hard to see."

After fifteen minutes, Pugh decides to pull his car to the north side of the house.

"There's an old burnt house there. I was going to try to get in that location where I could see the whole driveway and the house."

Pugh's instincts are working well. When he pulls his squad car back onto the road, he suddenly meets a green Blazer pulling out of the driveway that led to Carpenter's house. He recognizes the driver. It is Robert, Jr.

Pugh notices that the SUV has three occupants but he can't clearly see the other two people with Carpenter. He turns to pursue the Blazer, which immediately brakes to turn onto another road headed south. The detective flicks on his blue lights and in response the Blazer speeds up after it makes the right turn onto Franklin Road.

"I assumed at the time that Mrs. Lee was in the vehicle. I notified my dispatcher that I was going to back off. I didn't want them to wreck and she be hurt," he said later.

He just wants to keep them in his sights.

What the detective doesn't know — what he often would agonize about later, until an early death of a heart attack — was that while he was talking to the juveniles at the house half an hour earlier, Ann Lee was meeting her terrible fate at the end of the field road that ran back of the house towards the woods. All the young ones he talked to — teenagers and pre-teens — had outright lied.

"I don't know," Pugh would later lament on the witness stand and to his fellow officers more than once. "Maybe if I had gone up there behind the house I could've done something.

"I don't know."

That was just it. He had no way of knowing.

THREE

It's time to call the barn and let Ann know I'll be home in about an hour. I'll remind her that I'm going to take Dixie, our cat, to the vet for boarding.

Ann doesn't answer the phone. Instead it's one of her workers, Joe Williams, who picks up.

"Praise God, Bob," he shouts over the line.

Why does he say that?

"Ann's been kidnapped. You need to call the Collierville PD as soon as possible."

I am stunned. My stomach turns. I look up the number and call. A detective tells me it's true. They don't know her whereabouts. They're looking though. Several other law enforcement agencies are helping. He says he'll call me every ten minutes or so to update me.

He doesn't. But it's not his fault, of course.

Off the phone I try to take it in. This isn't happening. I don't believe this. What do I do? What did I do? As if it's my fault. I start to drive home. I hardly remember the drive. I'm trying to be calm. I'm checking every car along the way to be sure it isn't Ann's. My mouth is so dry. I can't swallow. I keep talking to God, or to myself. Or maybe both of us.

I make hasty calls to the children: "Your mom will probably be okay when they find her. Stay put until I know more."

I call Ann's good friend Carolyn. "I'll meet you at the house," she says. Numb, I keep driving, still checking every car I see in case Ann might be in it. Why is my mouth so dry?

In the driveway I see Carolyn's van. She's waiting for me.

Oh, God — what is happening to us?

* * *

Once the blue lights flip on above Pugh's cruiser, the driver of the green Blazer pushes the accelerator down as far as it will go.

"They were driving recklessly," Pugh recounted in the witness stand. "I just tried to keep them in sight. We approached speeds up to 100 miles per hour and higher. We were heading into Mississippi. I asked for some Marshall County units to meet me. I proceeded to follow."

As he pushes his cruiser to the limit, Pugh can see one or two faces peering back at him now and then. The road has numerous sharp curves. The Blazer winds all over the pavement and onto the shoulder, kicking up dust and gravel, skidding at turns, tires screeching. The vehicle speeds up when the road straightens. Luckily there are no oncoming vehicles.

"We were still on Franklin at this point," Pugh recalled in a court hearing, recounting dramatic circumstances in a calm and professional manner. "It becomes Clear Creek Road when you cross into Mississippi. First, though, we crossed U.S. 72 and went toward Holly Springs, Mississippi. At a location down there approximately four miles south of Highway 72, I lost my brakes on my squad car from the heat.

"They suddenly turned and I jerked in low, trying to make the turn. I couldn't. I slid through it. I was on gravel and I lost sight of the vehicle as I started to go more slowly down that gravel road."

Brakes or no, Pugh wasn't giving up on the chase.

Other police vehicles are approaching the area in a hurry. He radios where he had last seen the Blazer and guesses it could be picked up on South Slayden Road.

"That's where this gravel road runs out," Pugh said. "In a short period of time, I heard Investigator Ricky Wilson, who was coming from the Collierville area on U.S. 72, saying they spotted them coming out of South Slayden onto 72. The pursuit started again."

Pugh reaches U.S. 72. There he meets up with a line of various-colored squad cars, each car's lights flaring, sirens blaring, all coming from Slayden Road. Pugh's hot brakes are catching again by now and he finds himself in the middle of a fast-moving parade of screaming squad cars on the four-lane highway. People are standing outside the few businesses along the state highway, rubbernecking and pointing.

"We raced approximately half a mile east of an intersection where there's a store called Sharp's," Pugh continued.

Here the Blazer crosses the median once, twice, then exits the highway onto what appears to be a road that dead-ends into a wheat field.

"At this point I think there were 20 cars involved in the chase. There were about seven in front of me."

The entire police chase from 4680 Yager Road has covered 23 miles in less than 20 minutes on mostly narrow back roads. Now the Blazer is scrabbling on that rough ground, bouncing over ruts and cutting through half-grown weeds as the short, descending trail gives out at a fence line beside a pond and field of half-grown wheat.

Another pursuer remembered clouds of dust as cars careened into the field. The dust momentarily obscures the chasers' view of the Blazer, which doesn't stop until it reaches the fence and farm pond. There the vehicle stops suddenly, three doors spring open and three young men jump out and begin sprinting in various directions.

It is now every man for himself.

And the police pursuit has gone from rubber to leather.

Four

I have been home about four, long hours. No word yet on Ann. I am truly beside myself. I can't keep my head clear of terrible possibilities. I find it hard to catch my breath.

Finally one of the Collierville detectives calls and tells me, "Stay home. We're coming to talk to you."

A half hour goes by — achingly slowly. Finally, nine police and sheriff's cruisers pull into my long driveway. A police chaplain is with the officers. I say for the umpteenth time aloud or just in my head, no telling which, "Oh my God!"

I meet them outside in the driveway.

"I'm afraid, Mr. Lee, it's a homicide," one says. "We have two of the three men in custody."

My legs go weak and fail. Someone catches me. I look at the detective who spoke. "Let me kill them! Then you can kill me."

I mean it with all my heart.
I struggle to the house. Then I remember:
"What about Otis? He's always with Ann. Always."
"He's fine. He's at Detective Pugh's house."

* * *

It would be months later at a preliminary hearing that Bob Lee would finally hear exactly how the carjackers were caught. It would be when the medical examiner sat in the witness stand that he would hear the terrible details of Ann's ordeal that day.

That's how it is sometimes. The surviving family members are among the last to hear all the facts. Some bits they read in the press. Some pieces they pick up through a detective here or an assistant prosecutor there, or even through courthouse hangers-on.

But the need to know never leaves — not because it will change anything or make the pain go away — but because to know is to own your sorrow and your grief, to honor your loved one's memory, and to have a hope of working through your anger and your disgust. And maybe to begin to deal with what in the world to make, now, of your personal faith and life's very meaning.

Finally, there is that question, that terrible soul-searing challenge, that incredible, impossible concept people call *forgiveness*.

* * *

Captain Ricky Wilson was a 34-year-old Sheriff's investigator in 1999 when he joined the chase of the stolen green SUV. Pugh was his mentor and friend. In the witness box he described in matter-of-fact terms what was in fact a wild, two-state chase.

"Shortly after 3 o'clock Investigator Pugh spotted the Blazer that we were looking for. He gave chase. I was in Rossville at the time in an unmarked car. It's about a 15-minute drive at normal speed. I cut across Rossville at Highway 72 in Marshall County (Miss.) because that's the direction the pursuit was going.

"I was monitoring the chase on the Marshall County frequencies. They were making a lot of loops or switchbacks, back and forth on the median of 72. I finally caught up with them right there around Slayden Road. They actually crossed into the median at that time and so I drove into the median. Then they went back up the side of the median and crossed the highway, bouncing."

Returning to the scene 20 years later he added details he didn't have a chance to tell on the witness stand.

That section of Highway 72 had been rebuilt the year before. It has four smooth lanes, with a grass median as wide as the four lanes if lined up together. The median angles steeply down from each side of the roadbed so that at the bottom an SUV's roof would be about level with or even below the pavement.

Two decades later Wilson is older, heavier. Nonetheless, he recalls every detail in sharp, crisp focus.

"I topped a hill and I could see maybe a quarter of a mile away from me the Blazer coming toward me, cars in pursuit. That's when he dropped down into the median and I did the same on my side. I remember pulling my seatbelt as tight as I could because my intention was to hit them to stop them."

Both cars are grinding up grass and mud with their wheels as they barrel toward each other on the banked median. Just before Wilson can reach the Blazer, it turns and bounces up onto the highway, another police car right on its tail.

"I don't think they could even see if there was traffic or where they were headed," Wilson said. "They went up and crossed over the two lanes and right onto this short dirt farm road that happened to be there.

"David Cooke with the Marshall County Sheriff's Office was right on his tail. I suddenly found myself the number two car in the pursuit," Wilson said.

"The field road turned left. David's car was kicking up so much dust, gravel and bits of wheat that I couldn't see. There was a twenty-foot gully and I just missed it somehow."

The Mississippi Highway Patrol cruiser stays directly behind the Blazer, still churning loose debris into the air. Wilson maneuvers again behind that lead pursuit car as the Blazer turns onto a tractor path alongside a large field on the south side of the highway. A mild summer breeze lazily combs the top of the wheat.

At the end of the path, just short of a fence and pond, Wilson watches the occupants bail out of the Blazer and start running. He hits his brake pedal and gets ready to bail out, too.

Other pursuit cars come lurching to a halt in the dirt, sirens still sounding, blue lights casting a repeating 360-degree arc over the pond. Twenty-four officers almost jump simultaneously from 20 cruisers and unmarked vehicles, shouting to each other directions on which way the men have fled, and yelling commands at the three to halt.

Robert Carpenter, the skinny driver of the stolen SUV, runs wildly across the field, heading in an easterly direction. He falls once, gets up, and scampers on. Soon he is out of sight.

Eric Glover and Antonio Carpenter climb the farm fence and try to escape by way of the pond. Glover, the youngest, jumps into the water, and starts to wade across. He is caught by the time he climbs onto the man-made dam.

Antonio Carpenter, meanwhile, splashes through the pond's edge to a small feeder creek with four or five inches of water trickling toward the pond. He runs up the creek and into a patch of woods.

As the pursuit becomes a foot race, Wilson's eyes are on the driver. Robert Carpenter has sprinted to Wilson's left across the wheat field. Wilson and Cooke run after him. In their uniforms and heavy boots, weapons at their sides, they are no match for the fleeing teen.

"I know I was in better shape then and we hung with him for a little while. But Robert was nineteen and slim and we were carrying too many items — guns, bullets and the like — and extra pounds on our frames.

"As he started getting away from us, we pulled up and we both drew down on him. David Cooke and I talked about what happened next many times over the years. We didn't know each other then, had never met. But if we had known at that moment that Mrs. Lee was dead I think we likely would've shot him. We would've had every right at that point as he ran from us. Sometimes I wished we *had* fired.

"David looked at me and I looked at him. I said, 'Let's just shoot him in the ass.' But we didn't. We put our guns back and resumed running. He was pretty motivated, though, and not that many moments later we couldn't even see him. I mean — he was gone."

They follow on foot half a mile or so across the field but Carpenter disappears over a hill's crest. At the top of the hill they look around but don't see him. They lean over, hands on knees, gasping for air.

"Some people who lived in that area saw us. When he ran through their property that got their attention, and they saw us chasing him," Wilson later testified.

The two officers commandeer a four-wheel pickup from a resident and drive across more fields, trying to spot the suspect.

"He had a pretty fair head start on us at that point," Wilson said. "I was within probably twenty yards of him when he first got out of the truck, though."

Now, with nothing but hilly fields and woods in sight, the officers decide to return to the pond to see what has happened there and to organize a search for Robert Carpenter. When they reach the Blazer they find that Antonio Carpenter and Eric Glover are in custody, handcuffed and sitting quietly and glumly in the back of two patrol cars.

Neither had gotten far.

After Antonio climbed the fence, he splashed into the pond's edge, then loped up the creek bed to the woods. There, out of breath, he lay down in a small indentation beside the creek. Shadows alternated with streaks of light. Wet and exhausted in the day's heat, he apparently was hoping for camouflage.

Inexplicably, the younger suspect, Eric Glover, went straight into the middle of the pond. That slowed his progress.

As a dozen officers ran toward the woods, Detective Pugh and David Howell, of the Marshall County Sheriff's Office, climbed the fence and skirted the pond.

"A lady was fishing there. She yelled at us and pointed south of the pond's bank and we went that way," Pugh said. Just then they spotted a suspect starting to run on the levee above the pond, his clothes wet and slimy.

"It turned out to be Eric Glover. We did draw down on him at that time," Pugh succinctly testified.

To shouted orders, Glover drops to the ground. A Collierville Police officer dashes up, cuffs him and takes him into custody.

In the woods, meantime, Collierville Detective Gannon Hill and another officer, weapons drawn, have no trouble spotting Antonio on the ground, partially hidden behind a tree. He, too, is soaked from the pond and from perspiring and he is breathing heavily.

"He was lying down about five feet from the little creek bed that went through the woods there. We ordered him to show us his hands, at which time I placed him in handcuffs," Hill would say later.

As the two captives are marched, several yards apart, back to the cruisers, officers' hands gripping their arms, they are read their rights from a small card Hill always carries so he doesn't have to memorize the Miranda statement:

You have the right to remain silent. Anything you say can be and will be used against you in a court of law. You have the right to talk to a lawyer and have him present with you while you're being questioned. If you cannot afford to hire a lawyer, one will be appointed to represent you before any questioning if you wish. You may decide at any time to exercise these rights and not answer any questions or make any statements.

Hill explained later: "After the warnings are read we ask two questions. The first one is, do you understand each of the rights as I explained them to you? And having these rights in mind, do you wish to talk to us now?"

Neither captive speaks at first. Then Antonio Carpenter says they dropped "the lady" off along a road during the chase. He also blurts out that the other two had picked him up, and he had never seen the woman. The officers continue walking the two the 150 yards to the waiting cars. Tired and wet, heads lowered, the teens are searched and placed into patrol cars. In Anthony's pockets Major Randy Harper, of the Marshall County Sheriff's Office, finds $306 in cash.

The youngest of the teens — Eric Glover — is wearing brand-new Eddie Bauer clothes.

FIVE

Ann's friend Carolyn offers to go fetch Otis. I guess I must indicate that's okay, but I don't remember that later. She and her husband George leave. I walk into the house. Nadine, my sister-in-law, is there. She is Ann's sister. She goes to her house next door to get me a beer.

Some people start calling the house. I can't understand who it could be. How do they know? Then Dorene, one of our daughters, calls. She's on her way from Nashville. Bobby is leaving soon from Birmingham. One of them talks to Liz. She's coming as soon as she can catch a plane from New Mexico.

The beer doesn't taste good.

I just want water. I'm still so thirsty.

Carolyn and George come back with Otis. He looks bedraggled. I know he hasn't had his medicine for his epilepsy so I give him the pills. I sit on the floor and hug him.

I hug him like he's Ann. Or a part of her. Which he is.

All night long I don't know what to do with myself. This is a dream. No, it's a nightmare. I find a bucket and start mopping the kitchen floor for some reason. I know this doesn't make sense but I clean with intensity. The kitchen is Ann's room in the house more than mine. Is that why? I do it for what seems hours — mopping, scrubbing, dusting all over the kitchen. I stop and start all over again.

Maybe I just have to keep busy.

It's 1 a.m. Dorene arrives. I'm worried where everyone is going to sleep. We only have two bedrooms. My brother-in-law Otto opens up his travel trailer in his back yard.

It's the longest night. I keep asking anybody and everybody to confirm that Ann's really dead.

Isn't it a mistake?

* * *

Every officer in the Mississippi wheat field where the chase ended has one overriding concern: Where is Ann Lee?

Even as a search party is formed to find the one man still at large — and the other two are secured on the hard-metal back seats of cruisers — this question is topmost on everyone's mind. The scene is a bit chaotic as late afternoon shadows spread from a nearby stand of trees. Because several law enforcement agencies are involved, no one is in charge, technically. But without a discussion, all submit to Detective Chuck Pugh's direction. His demeanor and position seem to make him the leader. After all, he had started the chase, knew who he was chasing, and at least one of the perpetrators of the kidnapping lives in his Tennessee county.

The two handcuffed teens are at first questioned separately as they sit in soaked clothes in the back of patrol cars.

Pugh kneels at the open back door of the cruiser where 16-year-old Eric Terrell Glover has his head down.

Where's the lady you took — Mrs. Lee?

"I don't have any idea about any white woman."

Why did you all run from the vehicle when you stopped?

"No idea."

What's your name?

"Uh … Sincere Williams." He would keep claiming that fictitious name for the next two hours.

An officer from the Marshall County Sheriff's office walks up to Pugh from the Mississippi cruiser where Antonio Dewayne Carpenter is sitting and is being repeatedly asked questions.

"The other one says he's ready to tell you something," says Marshall County Detective Howell.

Pugh walks the few paces toward Carpenter, who has been taken out of the car. Two officers walk on either side of him. Carpenter sees Pugh and says loudly, "That lady's dead."

How?

"Robert beat her with a sawed-off gun."

Where is she?

"In the field up behind the house. The gun's there, too."

Pugh tells Carpenter to be specific about where he can find Ann Lee. Follow the dirt road behind the house until it ends and you will find her, the young man replies.

The fact that Carpenter had suddenly decided to talk would lead defending attorneys later to ask a lot of questions of officers in court about whether Carpenter was threatened to be "taken down the road" at any point.

With a sense of urgency now, Pugh and two other officers — Doug Davis and Tony Pace — get into their cruisers, maneuver back onto the highway and speed back to Yager Road.

"We did follow the old road up approximately three quarters of a mile off of Yager, back until it dead-ended into the woods," Pugh later testified in court.

An old farm road, photographed by police in 1999, began behind the Carpenter house and led almost a mile to the killing scene.

"It's just an old farm road. Like I say, you get up there and you just run out of anywhere to go.

"First thing I noticed was a big Schnauzer, laying down. When I noticed him, I stopped my patrol car and walked down to him. The dog lay there for a minute and then kind of run off. But where he was laying, I found the body of a white female in a ditch, in an indentation that had been covered up with — I thought it was horse blankets — and a large log and some bushes. It looked like an attempt to conceal the body."

Strewn around on the ground are a purse and various things taken from it — credit cards, bank receipts, Ann Lee's Tennessee driver's license and her mobile phone. They also find retail tags torn from the Eddie Bauer clothing. But they don't see the weapon.

Drag marks are visible. They lead from the road to where the body has been placed.

Pugh radios Ricky Wilson and tells him to ask Antonio exactly where the weapon is. Antonio, sitting again in the back of the police car in Mississippi, tells them to look fifteen meters away from the body. That terminology seemed strange and would be commented on many times later.

Fifteen *meters*.

Pugh remembers thinking: We're talking in feet, normally. "But when he said that I went — I want to say — west of the body. There was the gun. Pretty much fifteen meters away."

Its location would be measured precisely. The distance was fifty feet. Fifteen meters equals 49.21 feet. So the gun indeed was fifteen meters from where Ann Lee's body lay covered by the rugs, twigs and broken tree limbs.

Pugh settles in for the rest of the day at the Yager Road crime scene. He begins photographing and tagging as evidence the purse and items found on the ground. The coroner's office in adjacent Shelby County has been called. Dr. O.C. Smith will perform the autopsy.

Back in Mississippi it is nearly 6 p.m. As a dozen or more

officers have fanned off through fields to look for Robert Carpenter, Jr., his brother and cousin leave in a string of patrol cars headed to the Marshall County Jail in Holly Springs, Mississippi, 30 minutes away. They will be read their Miranda rights for a third time and be interrogated further.

When they arrive, still handcuffed and still wet and hot, an officer brings each a cold Coca-Cola. The handcuffs are removed and they are told to sit on metal folding chairs in a hallway. They don't say a word to each other. They stare at their shoes.

After determining Eric Glover's age, officers begin hunting for an adult relative who can come and be part of his questioning. Antonio Carpenter is taken to a room behind the jail. The room is simple, with more folding chairs and two tables.

Detective Ricky Wilson, Sgt. Glen Robinson observing, begins the questioning. It would be the first of three statements Wilson would take before the night is over. The clock will reach 3 a.m. before Wilson finishes the interviews and types his notes.

"To be honest I was still learning. I'd only been in investigations less than a year, but it came to me to question the three. I felt I could do it.

"By the time we got them settled at the Marshall County Sheriff's Office, Eric Glover wanted to talk right then and there. We got him to tell us his real name and we got his father to come. He was a pastor and that man was really torn up. He gave me permission to speak to Eric. He told him, 'Son, the only thing to do is to tell the truth now.'"

The statements Wilson would assemble that night will agree on many points, and diverge in some important ways. The statements were written down by hand, not tape-recorded. That

A police crime scene photo is a close-up of the rifle stock where it lay
after it was thrown by Robert Carpenter, Jr.

was customary at the Sheriffs' offices in 1999.

"I always begin with background questions — biographical,
education — and I asked whether he (Antonio) had taken any
alcohol or drugs in the past 24 hours," Wilson said. "He said he
hadn't."

Then the first interrogation goes straight to the crime.

Why are you here?

"It's about the lady who got car-jacked in Collierville."

Did you participate?

"No. I wasn't with them then. They picked me up later. I was
working on my car. When they came by with the lady and her dog
in her car I told Robert to let that lady go."

Did you touch the woman at all at any time?

"No."

How did she die?

"We drove to Yager Road and found out the police were

52

looking for Robert. He said he'd let her go but he hit her on the head with the rifle. Then he drove back where she was and drove over her four or five times."

You were in the car when the police were chasing it?

"I was in the back seat. That's all I know."

Wilson shows Antonio his statement and he signs it.

Then Anthony is put in a cell and Eric Glover is brought in. His father, Rev. James Wright, sits in on the session.

Eric is still ready to talk and his story carries the strong marks of detail and elaboration.

Earlier today you were in Collierville, Tennessee?

"Yes."

Who were you with?

"Antonio Carpenter and Robert Carpenter."

What were you doing?

"We were supposed to help work on Antonio's car. Antonio wasn't ready to get up so we were going to go to Sonic where our friend Mont works because he gives us free food. I got two chili dogs, a fry and a slush."

Where did you eat your food?

"In behind Sonic. Mont sneaks the food out the back door. Robert was parked on the side next to NAPA Auto Parts, sitting in his car waiting for me. When I finished eating I went back to Robert's car. The green Blazer was parked on the passenger side of Robert's car. When I came around the Blazer I saw the lady's dog. I think the dog's name was Otis. I asked the lady did it bite and she said no. Robert got out of the car with the sawed-off gun and went to her window. He told her to get to the other side. She tried to get out and he told her to get back here. She shut the door and he told her to shut up or he would shoot her. I got in the back of the Blazer and he told me to move his car to NAPA. I parked the car on the side next to Sycamore."

Describe the car to me.

"It's a Buick LeSabre. It's dark blue with a tan-colored top."

What did you do after you parked the car?

"Went to the Blazer. Gave Robert the key and went to get Antonio."

Where was the white lady at?

"Front passenger side."

What was she saying at this point?

"We could have her money. Just let her go."

Did you or any of the other two take any money?

"Robert took the money and gave it to Antonio."

How much was it that he took?

"A little over $300."

When you left Antonio's where did you go?

"Up to the train tracks and turned up through some factories. We went down to the road by the old milk barn and went into Fayette County. We went around by the big church by the highway and got on 57 Highway and went through Rossville. We turned on the road across from Troxel and went to Oak Grove and then to Yager. The lady was saying 'Let me out.' We were in the country. Robert wouldn't stop, though."

Where did you and the rest go then?

"Up the hill behind the house about a mile or so. We sat in the car and Robert said he couldn't let her go because she had seen his face. She told him she wouldn't tell. He then told her he wouldn't hurt her and told her to get out of the car. When he said that she said, 'You're going to kill me, aren't you?' She got out. I took her dog out. She asked me not to hurt him. I told her I wouldn't. Robert came around the back of the car while she was turned away and hit her in the back of the head with the gun. He hit her with the grip end of the gun. She went to the ground, kind of backwards and blood started coming from her head. She was moving around some. We threw her purse out and left back down the hill towards Robert's house. The kids stopped us and told us the police had just left. Robert turned around and took off fast up the hill."

How did he get back out to the lady?

"Through the woods. I was in the back seat. Robert came back to the lady and ran over her. He then backed up and ran over a second time. We got out and me and Tony started getting upset with him for running over her. We picked her up and all three of us carried her over and put her in a low spot and covered her up with seat covers and lumber."

Eric Glover and his father sign the statement as a true rendering of what Eric had said.

* * *

Several miles away, Robert Carpenter Jr.'s freedom is about to end. As officers search the fields, woods and occasional houses and barns, they come to one homestead that includes a scattering of old machinery and an abandoned car slowly rotting into the ground. They are nearly two miles from the pond where the Blazer ended the police chase. Four hours have gone by. Darkness is fast approaching.

Inside the rusting car, tucked down on the floor, Gannon Hill found Robert Carpenter, Jr. He too was wearing some of the

Eddie Bauer clothing. Officers describe Robert Carpenter as gloomy when they book him into the Marshal County Jail. Hill is removing Carpenter's handcuffs when he asks, "Do people who kill people go to hell?"

Hill doesn't respond.

"Well, I guess I'm going to go to hell because we killed that lady."

It is Robert Carpenter's turn to be interrogated by Detective Wilson. He is Mirandized a final time and asked formal questions about his name, where he lives, how far in school he has gotten. Has he had any drugs or alcohol in the last 24 hours? The answer is no. Then the questioning about the crime begins in earnest. Wilson's questions are informed by the earlier interrogations. Robert Carpenter's answers are brief. They include numerous inconsistencies.

Tell me why we are here.

"Me, Antonio Carpenter and Eric Glover took a car in Collierville and the lady in it when we took it got killed."

Tell me how she got killed.

"She got choked and then run over by her car."

Tell me how you got the lady's car.

"At the Sonic in Collierville."

Who was with you?

"Antonio and Eric."

How did you get in the car?

"I opened the driver's door and told her to get over."

Did you have a weapon?

"Yes. A sawed-off."

Where did you get it?

"In Byhalia from some guy named Mont who works at the Collierville Sonic."

Who got in the Blazer with you?

"Eric."

Where did Antonio go?

"He drove my car to NAPA and parked it."

After you left NAPA where did you go?

"Down Sycamore, went right down Keough through Rossville and went home down the road in front of Troxel."

Who was driving?

"Me."

Where was the lady sitting?

"Passenger seat in front."

Did she say anything to you?

"Yes. She asked if she could take her medicine. I told her yes."

Who took the money out of her purse?

"One of them in the back. It was $200."

Was the lady scared?

"Yes."

Why was she scared?

"She said she was scared we were going to kill her."

Did Antonio or Eric ask you to let her go?

"No. They asked what we were going to do with her. I told them I hadn't made up my mind."

Were you worried that she had seen your face?

"No."

Did she ask you to let her out?

"Yes. Several times."

Why didn't you?

"I was worried she would call the police."

When you got home did you speak to anyone?

"No."

Did you speak to your sister?

"No. I spoke to my brother LaMarcus."

Where was the lady sitting when he saw her?

"In the back."

Was she alive or dead then?

"Dead."

At what point did you kill her?

"Up the hill behind the house. … I didn't kill her."

After you killed her why did you load her into the truck?

"I didn't kill her. Antonio and Eric put her in there."

How was she killed?

"Choked with my gun and ran over."

Who choked her?

"They both did."

How did the lady come to be run over by the truck?

"I have nothing else to say about this."

* * *

No doubt Robert Carpenter realizes his answers are painting him into a bad corner. But Wilson remembers later there was another reason he quit talking.

"I had him. I really did. I think he was going to confess everything. You could just see the weight he was carrying. I had reached out and touched him on the shoulder at one point. Sometimes that's all it takes to get everything to come flowing out. But he hesitated and just then another officer walked into the room. His presence, his demeanor, changed the whole dynamic."

Wilson said the new officer was acting "bad cop" when that wasn't needed. "It was kind of one of those office politics moments. He was with another agency and for whatever reason he came in and stood, looking mean, arms crossed. The man's retired now and I won't name him. But I just will never forgive him for that. I was so close."

Robert Carpenter sits up straight, refuses to say more, and asks for a lawyer. But he signs off on the statement and he is placed in a cell.

The night is winding down at the jail adjacent to the sheriff's office. The three men had attempted to point fingers at each other. Some of what they said was true, some not.

At three in the morning, Wilson and another officer leave to find a bite to eat. Then Wilson drives to Collierville for a shower and two hours sleep. He has to be in New Albany, Mississippi, a 90-minute drive south of Memphis, at 8 a.m. for an extradition hearing for the three teens.

After a sleepless night in jail, the three captives will appear before a circuit judge and waive their extradition rights for transportation back to Tennessee. Eric Glover is transferred to Juvenile Court in Shelby County where he is held on an order signed by Fayette County General Sessions Judge Weber McCraw. He also is assigned a public defender. The brothers are taken to Somerville, Tennessee.

Now the slow, inexorable machinery of the justice system begins to turn.

SIX

It's 7 the next morning. Nadine brings me some coffee. The kids have all gotten a little sleep. We gather and wonder what we do now.

People start calling on the house phone at 8; workers from the barn, people we both knew, people only Ann knew. I can't handle taking calls. Dorene decides to handle that. She logs the calls.

Liz sits with me. Bobby sits, stands, sits again.

People want to know what they can do. I don't know. I'm amazed and confused about how many people are calling. I suddenly realize the news must be out. That hadn't occurred to me — that people would be hearing of Ann's death on the news.

I am beginning to feel angry. Guilty too. Why couldn't it have been me they killed? But mainly I'm starting to be consumed by anger. I can feel it, taste it. It's in my whole being. What I want to do is go and kill these men. I want vengeance. I don't care what it would mean for me. I express this to my children.

"Thanks, Dad," Bobby says. "Then we'd lose both of you."

I know he's right.

Some time that morning Big Joe comes from the horse barn where he worked for Ann and is outside raking leaves. Trying to be useful, I reckon. It's the last time I will ever see him. I will always wonder about him. He knew some of those killers.

Then some reporters and photographers start to come by. We let them come in. We want people to know what happened and to know what kind of person Ann is ... was.

Most of the time today my mind goes back to those men. I'm wondering how I can get to them. I really do want to kill them...

I go to the first hearing. It's now four long, exhausting days since Ann's murder. Liz goes with me. I have spent some time digging into my old combat training in the Army National Guard and then the Navy. I wonder: what ways could I get the bastards? Strong feelings of revenge fill my heart. For the first arraignment, I carry my firearm. I'm thinking of trying to get at least one of them in the courtroom before I can be stopped. But I leave the gun in the car.

At some of the hearings the defendants are always so close to me, especially in the old courthouse in Somerville where the early motions are held. I mean, really close! Nobody is even guarding them. Deputies stand over along one wall.

The men who took Ann's life are shackled, sitting in a nearby pew. Just a few feet away.

I always carry a thin Cross mechanical pencil with me. I know if I can get it into an eardrum I'd get the job done. At least

I can kill one of them before the sheriff's men can stop me.

How does someone plan a spouse's funeral when you don't have the body? This worry crowds in. The Shelby County Medical Examiner has the task to conduct an autopsy but the Fayette County Medical Examiner has custody of Ann's body. I have to petition for release of the body to a funeral home.

Ann and I talked a long time ago about whether we each wanted burial or cremation. Now I have to make a decision. I have to speak to the medical examiners' offices repeatedly. I speak to a funeral home and the church where we married. Things seem okay until I find that I have to pay the funeral home $2,000 upfront the very day that I'm trying to plan the funeral. I don't have that much in my account. My daughter Dorene says, "Don't worry, Dad, I'll pay for it."

Okay. Now, maybe, one day soon I'm going to find some time to actually grieve over Ann. But not while I've got to get back to court tomorrow.

* * *

Few people outside of court personnel, lawyers and journalists who cover the courts understand how the American legal system truly works — until they are caught up in it. This was true for Bob Lee. Over the next days and weeks he will grow confused and testy about how hearings are held and what happens or doesn't happen in court.

People who knew Bob Lee up to the time of the carjacking considered him a low-key and amiable man without anything striking or unusual in his appearance. He was a little shorter than medium and a little stouter than average. Everyone who knew him said he was hard-working, quick to laugh, happy to help anyone in need.

He had a soft voice that matched his manner. He also was known by friends and fellow workers as smart — supple with his hands and his brains.

After Ann's death, in the day, weeks, months ahead, the mild manner would disappear. The face that often smiled would grow taut with tension and anger. Even Bob has a hard time recognizing himself years later when he looks at newspaper photographs.

"I know that's me, but it's really not me. Do you know what I mean?" he asks a friend.

The day after Ann Lee's kidnapping and murder — June 16, 1999 — the three suspects waive extradition in Mississippi and are back north of the state line. Eric Glover is transported to juvenile detention in nearby Shelby County to await a hearing in five days. Gary Antrican of the Shelby County Public Defender's office speaks with him briefly before he is moved.

On June 17, the Carpenter brothers appear in Fayette County General Sessions court in Somerville on arraignment on a charge of first-degree murder. The Sheriff's Office also has charged them with carjacking and with counts of especially aggravated robbery and kidnapping. Both wear orange prison garb, with chains that wrap around their waists and ankles. They say little, shaking their heads when the judge asks if they can afford lawyers.

The two could be mistaken for twins. They wear their hair closely cropped, shaved above the ears. They mostly stare straight ahead as they sit on a scuffed courtroom bench in Somerville's old and quaint town square. They appear confused, but not scared. At later hearings the pair will alternately adopt defiant or bored appearances most of the time.

The murder warrants are signed by Chuck Pugh. The detective also has signed a report handed to the judge in which he gives initial details of the autopsy after talking with the medical examiner.

"Dr. (O.C.) Smith stated that the cause of death was from being crushed as a result of being run over by a vehicle," Pugh's report says. "He also stated that she had a crushed larynx from being choked with some type of round hard object, more than likely the barrel of the .22 rifle. Smith stated that this injury would have eventually caused her death but that she was still alive at the time she was run over. There were numerous other bruises on her body and a severe laceration to the top of the head."

More horrible details will come out later although exactly who did what to Barbara Ann Lee will never be known definitively — other than by the three attackers themselves.

The Carpenters are ordered held without bond.

Four days later, Eric Terrell Glover is in Fayette County General Sessions Court. His father is there with him. After some initial court business is handled, the courtroom is closed to the public and the press. Veteran reporter Tom Bailey, working for the Memphis daily newspaper, *The Commercial Appeal*, covers the proceedings inside the court when he can, and gathers information outside the court as the day's drama unfolds.

"Like the Carpenter brothers on Thursday," Bailey wrote for the next morning's front-page story, "Glover trudged into the Somerville courtroom Monday in an orange prison jumpsuit, leg chains and arm chains secured by a padlock hanging at the small of his back.

"The distraught-looking teenager sat on the front bench on

the right side of the courtroom, his head bowed," Bailey's detail-rich news story continued.

"On the front bench on the opposite side of the courtroom sat Lee, his daughter Liz Lee and some friends. They stared at Glover, with Robert Lee occasionally turning away only to shake his head in disgust."

The disgust soon will grow.

A little after 9 a.m. Judge McCraw walks into the courtroom and announces, in apparent irritation, that although the Fayette County District Attorney General's Office had been notified of the hearing, no prosecutor has shown up. McCraw appoints Detective Chuck Pugh to represent the State. He then orders members of the news media to leave the courtroom at the request of the defendant's temporary public defender, attorney Shana McCoy-Johnson.

For Bob Lee, this is too much. He jumps up and objects loudly. He wants the world to know what Glover has done. The judge listens calmly but sticks to his ruling and orders a $1 million bond, with a new hearing set for a week later to determine if Eric Glover should be tried as an adult.

Bob has moved from disbelief to outrage. He, with his small entourage, marches out of the courthouse and speaks to an assembly of news reporters before heading across the street to the county District Attorney General's office. Reporters scribble quickly as he talks. Broadcast reporters extend mikes. Cameras click or silently roll.

"I don't like the bond," he gruffly announces.

Never mind that Glover could never raise the amount of cash the bond would require.

"My wife was not allowed nothing! Those dastardly fools murdered my wife. I don't care if he (Glover) was six years old. My wife was 63 and those big men killed her. He's got more rights and more recourse than my wife did."

Bob's anger mounts higher. At the DA's office, he is only able to talk to a receptionist. The D.A., Elizabeth Rice, isn't in the office. His anger bursts onto the woman behind the reception desk:

"The State did not represent my wife's interest or mine," he yells, now livid. "I want her to call me right now. I want to be notified on what's going on in the prosecution of my wife's murder."

Bob is shaking, red in the face. Finally, his daughter Liz and Susan Gillpatrick of the Shelby County Victims Assistance Center are able to pull him away.

He asks them what's going to happen the next day when the two brothers are in a hearing. "This is a travesty," he thunders.

* * *

Years later, Bob recalls that day with a mix of wonder and embarrassment at his own naiveté.

"The judge asked in court where the DA was. No one seemed to know. Eric stood there in chains. I could only imagine that they were going to let him go because most courts — that is, in traffic court — dismiss charges when no one representing the state shows up. That's why I stood up and objected to the whole proceedings."

What Bob doesn't realize is a tug-of-war concerning the presence of lawyers at hearings has been going on for a while between the judge and the prosecutor's office.

Bob stares into middle space, reliving the day and his emotions in vivid color.

"The judge was very understanding and quietly asked me to sit down."

Later that day, Attorney General Rice calls Bob. She explains that she is short on prosecutors — a problem she and Judge McCraw have been feuding about for months. Her prosecutors had other hearings that day, and the bond hearing for Glover was preliminary. There would be more hearings and more chances for the facts to come out.

"I really appreciated her call. I needed to sit back a little. Of course, later on I would listen to some testimony in court and think it didn't go far enough or I'd want more to come out and get angry all over again. I just didn't understand what was going on, why lawyers were doing what they were doing. All the motions, the repeated hearings. I went to every single court hearing. It seemed endless and often senseless to me."

Things will become ever more complicated as the federal government also begins proceedings across county and jurisdictional lines. Questions arise. Which authority has priority? Who will take the lead — the state or the federal prosecutors? If both the feds and the state hold trials separately, will that constitute double jeopardy for the defendants?

Fortunately for Bob, some lawyers, including prosecutors, later are willing to take time to explain what is happening in and out of court and what the motions all mean.

Even better, an advocate for the families of homicide victims will be with him practically every step of the way.

* * *

Susan Gillpatrick was hired the year before Ann's death as Shelby County, Tennessee's first victims' family advocate and counselor.[ii] The tireless social worker labored with the homicide response program.

"We would call on the family members of everyone killed in Shelby County, introduce ourselves, offer help. We would do things such as filling out paper work, keeping them informed of court dates, and listening to their thoughts and fears," she recounts.

"I would meet with people wherever was necessary — at home, at work, at school. After a while we even had calls from cases that had occurred 10 years prior. They'd hear about the program, call and ask for counseling or help with victim impact statements."

She met with Bob and his family soon after Ann's murder. Two decades later she vividly remembers it as a complex situation. Immediate family members were living in different states, various jurisdictions were involved, and the potential of trials in two or more courts loomed in the future for the Lee family.

"I knew theirs was an overwhelming situation. In the first place, families aren't expecting such terrible news. And if you don't work in the legal system you don't know what to expect: the tactics lawyers use, but also the fabrications and even the lies that come out about your loved one.

"I met with them very early after the homicide. I met them in their home. I spent a lot of time, helping them get through each day. A lot of emotional support is needed.

"Sometimes it's the little things. Twenty years ago we didn't have electronic files. I would cut out every single newspaper article and bring them newspaper clippings. I remember going into the living room one day and the pile of newspaper clippings looked like a phone book.

"Early on I gave them a pen and notepad and told them to write down everything. If they get a call about a court date, write it down. If they wake up in the middle of the night with a burning question, write it down.

"It gives some sense of control when you don't have much or any control over the process and the outcome."

She says of Bob Lee and his family, "They were good people whose lives were just blown away in all aspects by Ann's homicide. Losing Ann was the primary loss but other losses came with it in the new roles for family members, in all the ways life suddenly changes. And in the wider community, especially in horse circles, Ann was known and loved and so the loss existed in that sense too.

"Somehow, through it all Bob kept his sense of balance. I know he was so angry and felt so helpless, especially at the beginning. But even at his angriest he was still in control of himself. He's a remarkable man and I loved working with that family."

For his part, Bob Lee remembers wondering how he and his children could have gotten through those early days if they hadn't had Susan's knowledge and understanding to lean on.

Susan left the job after three years and began a career as a crisis manager.

"It got to be too much for me," she explains.

"It was a 24/7 life. I would go to bed knowing and thinking about who had been killed that day. I would get up the next morning, watch television news and read the newspaper and begin contacting new families. I'd say 99% of them wanted to meet with me. Dealing with the terrible consequences of homicides every day — it just never goes away."

The terrible, jumbled, nightmarish month of June, 1999, finally comes to a merciful close. Bob learns that two separate sovereign government domains — the State of Tennessee and the United States of America — have the right to determine the guilt or innocence of the defendants and to hold the guilty parties accountable. There exists no double jeopardy in doing so. The case will proceed on two parallel courses.

One thing is certain: federal and state prosecutors are eager to try the cases.

SEVEN

The days and the weeks go by. It's such a hot summer. I'm in a fog much of the time. A state of shock, I suppose. But now and then life takes on some clarity. Then the clouds return.

I find I have nearly forgotten that I have a job; that I was someone who used to work for a living. I go whole days without that even crossing my mind. Thank God for the managers at the casino. They never talk to me about coming back to work. When I finally do drive to my job, more than a month later, they send me to the personnel office to get my family leave. "Come back when you're ready," they tell me. "The job will be here for you."

It reminds me there are good people in the world. Their generosity makes a big difference.

I try to tune in to myself. For the first time in my life I'm developing ulcers and I have gout. I had shingles once and now it comes back worse than before. I don't seem to be able to lose weight, though.

One day I recognize that I'm depressed. My family and friends push me to get counseling. I talk to a couple of psychologists and I even see a psychiatrist. I go once a week for the time my insurance will cover to see one psychologist. She's helpful. But the psychiatrist is a waste of time and money. I go in once or twice a month. He sits at his computer and asks, "What are you feeling now?" I start talking. It goes 12 minutes — the time allowed per session by insurance. Then he hands me a prescription. No conversation. I soon decide that's a waste in every way.

My life otherwise is an endless round of trips to courtrooms to witness the filing of motion after motion by what seems like a long line of lawyers coming and going. It's interesting to me for some reason that I live about halfway between the Fayette County Courthouse in Somerville and the U.S. Federal Courthouse in downtown Memphis.

I every day want to get to the actual trials. Can we have a trial for these murderers? Please?

My family is a rock, at least. My children take turns taking care of my home and daily needs. They remind me of the things Susan has told me.

I look for any chance to talk to reporters. I don't care if someone wants to call me a camera hog. Any time I can keep them from talking to the brothers, the killers, is good. People ask me, "Why do you want all this publicity?" Well, I sure don't want the bad guys to get all the attention.

One day several months later, the federal judge assigned to the case, Jon McCalla, is reprimanded for reprimanding an attorney or two. That's how it seems to me. A television reporter calls me. I'm actually not too sophisticated about interviews. I tend to think it's just the two of us having a conversation. I tell her, "If you ask me, some of those attorneys need haranguing."

That makes news.

Do I care? No, not really.

All I want is to see some justice for Ann.

* * *

Seven days have inched by for Bob since Ann Lee was kidnapped and slain. It is June 22, 1999. Separate legal actions occur this day in Memphis and in Somerville. These are early days for the case and many steps must occur through the justice systems before a trial can begin — an agonizing wait for the Lee Family.

The federal grand jury convenes in downtown Memphis and issues indictments of brothers Robert and Antonio Carpenter on three counts each of carjacking, the killing of a witness to a federal crime (the murder of Ann herself), and the use of a firearm in a crime of violence. The first two offenses carry the potential penalty of life imprisonment, or death, under a federal omnibus crime bill passed by Congress only five years earlier.

Grand jury proceedings are secret. No other information is forthcoming, except that Assistant U.S. Attorney Tony Arvin explains outside court that no indictment was handed down against Eric Glover because the federal prosecution of juveniles is difficult. The sixteen-year-old's future will be left in the hands of State prosecutors and a jury of people living in Fayette County and nearby counties.

That afternoon Fayette County Judge McCraw holds another hearing. This will be the first chance for Bob to see the Carpenter brothers. In court he stares at them as if he can make them feel his pain and anger. The session is brief and most of the action is up at the bench. McCraw appoints lawyer Tom Minor to represent Antonio. He intends to name Richard Rosser to defend Robert, but Rosser points out conflicts of interest and so the judge says he will appoint someone else soon.

"My wife knew the lady who got killed," Rosser explains afterward. He also tells of a distant family relationship to the victim.

Someone from the DA's office attends today's hearing. Assistant District Attorney Walt Freeland participates in the discussions and confers on the side with Bob and his daughter Liz.

It will be more than a month before the Fayette County Grand Jury can convene to consider indictments based on Fayette Sheriff Bill Kelley's charges of murder, carjacking, aggravated robbery and kidnapping. Although little has happened in court this day, Freeland's information and personality help Bob feel like the system may be starting to work. The earlier phone conversation with D.A. Rice helped too.

He doesn't understand the nature of the D.A.'s apparent disagreement with the judge but is satisfied that his concerns have been heard at this point.

In fact, the ongoing argument between Rice and McCraw affects much of the Fayette County legal environment. McCraw doesn't like to hold court without prosecutors present; Rice says there are more hearing dates than her small stable of prosecutors can cover in Fayette and the other four counties in her jurisdiction. The dispute threatens to get personal.

Several other district attorneys across the state have been complaining about budgets too small to hire needed prosecutors.

Rice says she must weigh the importance of every session in the various courtrooms, so assistant D.A.s are assigned to McCraw only six days of each month.

Despite the disagreement, the two work out a schedule. McCraw has been on the Sessions Court bench since 1990. In 2005 he will be appointed to the 25th Judicial District Circuit Court in Somerville by Gov. Phil Bredesen, taking the seat of retiring Judge Jon Kerry Blackwood.

Four years before that happens, Blackwood will be the judge in the actual state murder trials of the Carpenters and Glover.

McCraw adjourns court after setting a probable-cause hearing one week hence for all three defendants. At the next session he will hear arguments about whether Glover should be tried as an adult. The defendants are sent back to the Fayette County Jail. Soon they will be transferred to a jail in another Tennessee county for security reasons.

That move later will prove to be a mistake.

As the days go by, newspaper letter-writers begin airing their feelings of anger and dismay. The case has conjured many area residents' fears about crime and the widespread belief that criminal justice is too often lacking for victims and their families.

"I have heard as much as I can stand," writes one woman to *The Commercial Appeal* in a typical letter to the editor. "Why are repeat offenders let off time after time? Why can't we even feel safe eating lunch anymore? Why was there no prosecutor at the hearing?"

"I am a firm believer in executions," another writes. "Some people say executions are not a deterrent but I believe they would be if we would just carry them out quickly."

Many residents of Collierville, as in other nearby suburban areas, are decrying the specific Lee crime and the seemingly mounting crime rate that some say is the result of over-development, urban sprawl and population growth. Many ask in writing to newspapers and vocally on local radio talk shows if they can feel safe at home or while shopping anymore.

* * *

When Judge McCraw reconvenes court on June 29 the purpose is a preliminary hearing about juvenile Eric Glover's status as a defendant. A closed-door session takes place. The verdict: Glover will be tried as an adult along with the Carpenter brothers.

Robert Carpenter now has an attorney named Stephen Hale in the state case. Hale enters a motion asking for an independent psychiatric examination of Robert to determine if he's competent to stand trial. McCraw quickly denies the motion.

Hale says outside the courtroom he will make the same request as soon as he can to the trial judge, Fayette County Circuit Court Judge Blackwood. In coming days, when state prosecutors request a test for competency, Hale will find himself squarely at odds with other lawyers.

All three young men are bound over to the next session of the Fayette County Grand Jury. That body begins its work July 26.

Another week crawls by. The complicated and seemingly repetitious process agonizes Bob Lee. He attends a hearing in downtown Memphis where U.S. Magistrate Diane K. Vescovo seeks information on the Carpenters' assets to determine whether the government should grant them legal service at no charge. Each briefly takes the stand. Antonio says he owns nothing. Robert tells

Vescovo he owns a 1987 Buick LeSabre.

"The government will provide attorneys," she rules.

Assistant U.S. Attorney Arvin asks that no bond be set for the brothers. A hearing on that question and other matters will be held in two days. It's Wednesday afternoon now. Bob heads home to beat rush-hour traffic and to await the next journey to court on Friday.

At the Friday procedural hearing, one theme overshadows all others. Vescovo asks the key question.

"Is the Government pursuing the death penalty?"

"We *are* pursuing that avenue," Tony Arvin responds.

Then the judge turns to the question of the brothers' defense. She explains they are both allowed two lawyers and at least one must have death penalty experience. Federal public defender Stephen Shankman is now working for Robert in what seems to be a fast-moving federal case. A second lawyer will be appointed for him and two for Antonio, Vescovo promises.

The federal prosecution's intention to try the brothers under the death penalty takes the case into fairly rare territory. Since the 1995 national crime bill, only 69 such cases have been approved for the death penalty in 243 federal homicide prosecutions through 1999.[iii]

Bob also learns that a federal trial may be held before a state trial. He tells reporters about that outside court. Bob is getting a feel for how to work with the news media.

In court that day Robert Carpenter waives his right to a detention hearing, which is considered a pro-forma legal step. Antonio's detention question is delayed until he's properly "lawyered-up." After the hearing, prosecutor Tony Arvin explains to Bob that he will submit a death penalty request to the U.S. Department of Justice but he will need the family's help.

* * *

I think about the crime and the Hell she must have gone through many times a day.

So writes Liz Lee about her mother in a letter dated July 17 to U.S. Attorney General Janet Reno in Washington, D.C. Liz, who travels all summer back and forth from New Mexico, has worked hard on the letter. She feels much will be riding on what she says:

I can't put it to rest because she didn't just die, she was brutally murdered. I haven't had time to grieve because of all the hearings and trials to come. There will not even begin to be a closure for some time ...

The impact this has had on the rest of my family is equally as devastating. All of us (are) having to seek counseling and support to try to deal with this tragedy. Not to mention the travel expenses and lost wages we are all incurring. All this we would not be doing if they had just let her go. I wouldn't be writing this Impact Statement if they had let her go unharmed, but they didn't.

They made a conscious, deliberate decision to kill her and they need to pay for that decision.

If we are going to have the Death Penalty as a punishment for certain crimes, then tell me who better deserves this sentence than someone who could commit such a brutal crime as Robert Carpenter, Antonio Carpenter, and Eric Glover did?

* * *

Several more weeks will go by before Janet Reno will make her decision in time for a trial. She will first receive an opinion from a panel of Justice Department executive employees. At the family's request, several people who knew Ann Lee in Collierville, Germantown and the surrounding county also write letters to Reno. Bob and his family now feel they have done what they can to get what they see as ultimate justice for their wife and mom in the federal court system. But they vow to stay on top of the process, day by day, hour by hour.

Meanwhile a new U.S. hearing is scheduled for Monday, July 26. It is for discussions and rulings on more procedures and motions.

The day opens with thunderstorms crackling through Shelby County, as hot winds from the west strike a cooler front entering the Mid-South from the north. The storm is over by 10 a.m. Now the humidity threatens to match the day's high temperature mark, which flirts with 90 degrees.

Heat of another kind seeps into a downtown Memphis hearing room as federal defense attorneys bring complaints about the state trial before Federal Magistrate Vescovo. Attorney Robert Hutton speaks for the four lawyers now working for the Carpenters.

"They have no right to talk to our clients," Hutton argues forcefully about state prosecutors and their plans to have psychiatric evaluations performed on the brothers. Defense attorney Hale, still working in the state case, has happily agreed to the evaluations.

Although physically the two Carpenters are in state custody, they technically are being held in the custody of the federal system for now. Hutton wants to keep that status quo.

As the judge listens, Hutton continues his complaint. He

wants Magistrate Vescovo to prohibit the state from seeking the evaluations.

"It will impact the fairness of the trial in this court," he assures her.

Antonio's two lawyers are Howard Wagerman and James Simmons. They say they agree with Hutton. Vescovo moves cautiously.

"You certainly have raised serious matters at this early point in the case," she says. She gives lawyers until 4 p.m. the next day to put their arguments in writing. Before the hearing is over the Carpenter brothers formally plead not guilty to the federal charges.

It is a full day, meantime, in Fayette County where the grand jury has been convened and announces indictments against all three defendants on four counts: premeditated first degree murder, felony first degree murder, especially aggravated kidnapping and especially aggravated robbery. Whether the death penalty will be sought by the state is as yet not certain. Judge Blackwood now has the case in his court.

The Carpenters and Glover will be arraigned on the charges the next morning.

As these events are going on, phone conversations are held among various attorneys about the objections made by Hutton. Hale, Robert's lawyer in the state case, soon agrees to coordinate with William Massey, Robert's second lawyer in federal court, and to set aside his agreement for now on the state prosecutor's request of a psych exam. State and federal prosecutors confer as well. By day's end, the number of defense lawyers in both jurisdictions will be whittled to four.

The next day, an unusual court hearing is held in a small room of the U.S. Courthouse in downtown Memphis.

U.S. District Judge Jon McCalla, who will adjudicate the federal case, has been handed the reins by Vescovo. McCalla is out of town but holds the hearing by phone. The Carpenters, U.S. prosecutor Arvin, and four defense lawyers form a half circle in front of a speaker phone sitting on a table. Everyone leans in close to hear the judge. A few paces away, journalists and Bob Lee are doing their best to hear what is said.

McCalla is glad to learn that the lawyers have worked out the potential conflict between the state and federal jurisdictions. He points out this will be his first death penalty case as a jurist if Reno so rules. The telephone hearing is civil and brief.

In keeping with the oral settlement of the psychological testing question, Fayette Judge Blackwood rules the following day that evaluations of Robert and Antonio to determine mental competency to stand trial are on hold. But the judge lets stay his ruling in one part. He wants the Carpenters' intelligence quotients to be measured at the local J.B. Summers Counseling Center. Because the federal prosecution doesn't include Eric Glover, McCraw's ruling directing a full series of evaluations of the 16-year-old remains in force.

Nevertheless, like the summer thunderstorm that had moved rapidly today through West Tennessee, leaving behind a steamy and sticky afternoon, the legal storm is over. At least for now.

* * *

The blazing summer of 1999 meanders on until a bit of unexpected drama in the West Tennessee town of Brownsville in August interrupts the days between courtroom visits for the Lee family.

What happens would seem to fit better as a plot in a fictional TV police drama than in real life.

Brownsville is the county seat of Haywood County 54 miles northeast of Memphis. A jailhouse there adjacent to the Sheriff's office had been "home" for Robert and Antonio Carpenter since soon after they were captured in June. The jail — about as old and in need of replacement as the one in Somerville — had been deemed "somewhat more" secure by Fayette County authorities. Brownsville also had an available cell the brothers could share while awaiting their trials.

It is about 6:30 p.m. on Sunday, August 8, 1999. The jail is as quiet as it ever is. Meals have been served. Some prisoners are out of their cells, reading books, watching TV or chatting in the corridor. A jailer is moving through the long hallway, sending inmates to their cells for the night.

When he comes to Robert and Antonio — both are nonchalantly leaning against the wall — the brothers jump the guard and wrestle him to the floor. The jailer hurts his head. The brothers grab his keys, and quickly open a door to an outside yard.

The jailer is dazed but not badly injured. Another jailer catches the escape attempt on a video monitor in the sheriff's office, radios for help and starts a facility lock-down.

In the yard the Carpenters — once more this summer they are attempting to flee pursuing authorities — look for a place to scale the fence. Now other guards are answering the alarm, so the teens decide instead to climb to the jail's roof in search of a way out.

That is as far as they are going to get.

Several deputies corner the two on the roof within minutes,

weapons drawn. The brothers meekly surrender and are placed in solitary confinement. They will be formally charged with attempted escape.

The next day the Haywood County Sheriff's Office informs Fayette County the brothers are no longer welcome in Brownsville. The Carpenters are transferred back to Somerville where they are separated.

Each now is in a cell with another prisoner. They have spent their last night in a cell together.

"It was one more nightmare," Bob Lee recalls 20 years later. "That these two could even get close to escaping was almost too much for me to handle. How can that happen? Again I wondered if we were going to get justice."

Chuck Pugh, the Fayette Sheriff's investigator who knew the brothers and had first given chase back in June on the day of the kidnapping and murder, proves more philosophical about it in interviews with reporters at the time.

"These boys have nothing to lose by trying to escape or hurting anybody," he tells a reporter. "After all, they are looking at the real possibility of two death sentences."

* * *

As summer turns toward fall, the wheels of justice — in U.S. District Court for the Western Division of Tennessee and in Fayette County District Court of Tennessee — are now churning at a steady pace even if progress mostly is invisible to the public and incessantly slow and grinding to the Lee family. Standard legal procedures must be followed. Evidence must be gathered, including lab test results. Arguments based on evidence and how evidence may be weighed by juries must be considered, particularly by the defense. Lawyers are busy collecting information and fill white boards with potential arguments.

The question of whether to seek the death penalty for Robert and Antonio Carpenter remains alive for both prosecutions. Eric Glover, however, who will soon turn 17, won't face death, state District Attorney General Rice decides.

The first decision about the Carpenters comes in early September. Rice announces her prosecutor, Assistant D.A. Walt Freeland, *will* seek a death sentence for the brothers. On the federal side, more officials are involved in the decision that ultimately rests with Janet Reno. Prosecutor Arvin must send his recommendation to Washington, D.C., before the end of September. Defense attorneys will send their arguments opposed to capital punishment.

FBI lab tests on two dozen pieces of evidence from the case also are pending. Results mainly will prove helpful in the sentencing phase of the trials. Both sides need to see those results. A full pathology report has yet to be released from the medical examiner's office, too.

Judge McCalla sets a November trial date. He allows two weeks on the calendar and says the trial won't be moved from Memphis and he's disinclined to seclude the jury. Arvin says he can meet that deadline for trial but the defense attorneys say they are less sure they can be ready.

McCalla sternly issues some directives to the lawyers: move at a "crisp" and "steady" pace; don't give interviews to the press; don't throw good judgment out the window in the number of witnesses brought to court.

Behind the scenes, the Justice Department's special death

penalty panel looking at the question of a capital trial does recommend the ultimate penalty. The final decision is expected soon from Reno. Will the death penalty and the potential of federal executions be in play?

* * *

Defense lawyers begin to refine their lines of attack. One is made public on the 25th of September. Robert's attorneys pounce on the state's death penalty notice, filing a motion in Somerville seeking to prevent capital punishment on racial grounds.

Robert Hutton and William Massey accuse Rice of having engaged in a "pattern and practice while district attorney of racial discrimination by seeking to impose the death penalty only upon African American citizens."

The lawyers had been busy. They had assigned an investigator to thumb through documents in the Tennessee Administrative Office of the Courts in Nashville to prove the claim. The statistics seem overwhelming. Of 23 cases in Rice's jurisdiction since 1995 in which the death penalty was sought, all were African American defendants.

It becomes obvious that the main defense aim is to prevent a death sentence in the case, now divided into two separate state trials by jury for the three defendants and set to begin November 15. It's the same date set by Judge McCalla for trial to begin in federal court.

At home, Bob Lee and his family are seething about the defense motion. His daughter Liz writes a letter to the newspaper: "It sickens me that the murder of my mother is being turned into a racial issue."

The question of race has largely been ignored, at least

publicly, since the day Ann Lee was killed. The word "thugs" has been used often to describe the suspects but that isn't yet seen as the racially-charged word it will be considered almost universally in American life in the 21st century.

* * *

Fall weather arrives late in autumn 1999 in West Tennessee. Days stay hot into October. The winter holidays are weeks away but the approaching new year is a major subject of discussion and worry throughout the world

Although the next year, 2000, actually is the last year of the 20th century and not the first year of the next, a millennium fever has gone global. One question is on a lot of minds: will computers continue working as they should after December 31, 1999? Or will the millennial turn of calendars to 00 interrupt computer networks and operating systems? Governments and corporations worry especially about banks and other financial networks, the Social Security and Medicare systems, food distribution centers and national security.

It is almost inevitable that the trial dates will be rescheduled as lawyers file motions and seek more time to build a defense. Even Bob Lee accepts that fact. On November 10 defense lawyers seek subpoenas of state law enforcement records to support their racial discrimination claim. There will be procedural hearings, but a trial date now is set for March, 2000.

Bob Lee is happy to tell reporters what he thinks after spending most of a day attending one long hearing in Somerville December 15.

"It's not a question of *whether* they did it," he says, looking at reporters. "It's a question of *what century* they're going to be tried in."

The Fayette County hearing this day is for the purpose of arguments on dozens of filed motions. It is the proverbial pinnacle of pre-trial proceedings — one that will last several hours.

Defense attorneys for both Carpenter brothers put one request after another before Judge Blackwell. State's attorneys have their responses prepared. The Lee family doesn't know it, but many are routine pre-trial motions brought forward in most violent felony cases by defense attorneys during early proceedings.

In the process, lawyers for both sides begin to reveal the cards they hold. The judge shows how much leeway he is likely to allow at trial.

A total of eight lawyers — four per side — take their seats at the tables in the front of the courtroom. Representing D.A. Elizabeth Rice's office are Assistant D.A.s Walt Freeland and Colin A. Campbell. Representing the State Attorney General's Office are Michael Meyer and David M. Himmelreich. Antonio Carpenter's defense lawyers are Howard L. Wagerman and Jim Simmons. Appearing on behalf of Robert Carpenter are William D. Massey and Robert Hutton.

The day's proceedings will fill 174 official recorded pages typed by court reporter Andrea Meyers.

A first motion before the court seeks to quash subpoenas by the defense that would call D.A. Rice and a representative of the Tennessee Bureau of Investigation into court — with documents — to explain their "charging" decisions. This is part of the defense fight against the death penalty. State attorneys use the state's code of laws and past court decisions to argue why the judge should disallow the subpoenas. Meyer argues for the quash for twenty-five minutes.

Speaking for Robert Carpenter, Hutton follows Meyer by immediately going to the reason for the subpoenas.

"If your honor please ... the State is seeking the death penalty. We filed a motion stating that there has been a pattern in practice of racial discrimination" within the 25th Judicial District of Tennessee. Rice, he says, has sought the death penalty only against minority defendants. He says there are at least two "similarly situated" egregious cases against white defendants where the death penalty wasn't sought. He argues the defense motion is to help prove the facts.

Hutton points out one infamous case that occurred in nearby Hardeman County in September, 1992. Dennis Harris, then thirty-four, of Bolivar, Tennessee, was charged with first-degree murder, robbery and arson in the killing of six poker players. The trial occurred in 1995.

"Your Honor," Hutton says, "that was a white defendant in this district who shot a man and burned five men alive. He had one shot, the others tied up, oil poured on them; <they were> burned alive in their own house, which is clearly heinous, atrocious and cruel. It's mass murder. It was murder in the perpetration of robbery."

In that case, he says, the district attorney didn't even seek life without parole let alone the death penalty. He adds, "Yes, we do want to subpoena the District Attorney General. We want to put her on that stand and make her explain why she's only sought the death penalty against African Americans and not against White defendants."

At this point David Himmelreich, the state's Deputy

Attorney General, stands to speak, taking "great exception" to Hutton's claim. He says the defense hasn't done its homework, hasn't looked at enough records.

"What they've done is go back to about 1995 on a computer … and found a couple of cases where white persons were not charged with the death penalty," he says. He also says some D.A. and TBI files should remain confidential and lists several reasons and laws to support his argument.

When he finishes, the hearing turns back to Hutton, who tells the judge he simply wants to "point out to the Court the ludicrousness of the State's position" on a statute Himmelreich used in his argument.

Now comes Simmons, attorney for Antonio Carpenter, making it clear that his client joins in Hutton's argument. Another 22 minutes have gone by.

Judge Blackwell speaks. He tells the room of lawyers and spectators that he has spent a lot of time thinking about the particular motion since it was first filed. He spent most of the previous evening reviewing one case on record brought up by the defense. Then Blackwell says, "I have been the presiding judge in nearly every case (in which) Ms. Rice has sought the death penalty." He further states he's not certain about a legal definition of "similarly situated" when it comes to comparing individual cases.

Then he gives his decision: he will quash the subpoenas for files from the TBI and D.A.'s office and the attempt to put Rice in the witness stand. But he will allow the defense to seek more files from the court clerks and the sheriff's departments in the district's counties.

The next motion, announces William Massey, is about discovery of information both sides may have and showing that the two sides have agreed to follow Rule 16 in judicial proceedings. The rule guarantees the sharing of facts and evidence. So ordered, the Judge says.

Then Wagerman stands on behalf of Antonio Carpenter. "We've got a separate set of motions but some overlap ... do you want us to jump on up like I'm doing now and be heard?" Some in the courtroom laugh at that and Blackwell tells him he may do so.

What follows is a discussion on several legal steps to which attorneys typically agree concerning evidentiary discovery, shared lists of witnesses and the suppression of some photos taken by investigators at the scene of the crime. The judge quickly assents to matters the various lawyers have agreed to, including considering before the trials the impact of pre-trial publicity. A change of venue motion will be tabled until the trial dates are closer.

Attorneys for the Carpenters announce they will withhold a motion that the death penalty be declared unconstitutional and will keep it for "appellate purposes."

"That motion will be denied" in his courtroom, Judge Blackwell says, as will be another motion seeking any sentence other than death. A motion seeking a hearing about whether Robert Carpenter is "mentally retarded" and ineligible for the death penalty is set aside temporarily by the judge.

Then Massey stands to address the court.

"We have a motion to dismiss the indictments due to racial and gender discrimination in the selection of the grand jury forepersons," he says. "I believe it's going to take a little bit of argument."

It is at this point in the hearing that Bob Lee finds it difficult to remain seated and quiet. He is exasperated. He feels the old anger rising.

"I'm thinking," he remembers years later, "there is so much dumb crap going on. When can we get to actually trying those men?"

But Robert Carpenter's lawyers are serious about bringing more facts into the hearing. All the defense lawyers believe they have, after all, a narrow legal lane before them that amounts to trying to save their clients' lives once they likely are convicted on the charges.

Hutton says he wants to prove in court that women have been approximately 50 percent of the population in Fayette County, Tennessee, for more than a century — and that black persons often have made up the majority of the population over that time — and yet "all the grand jury forepersons have been white males since 1870."

And he asks the State's attorneys to stipulate to those facts.

Says Freeland, "Your Honor, I don't think I can stipulate as to facts prior to my birth."

Blackwell reserves that motion for later in the day. Then the lawyers converse for nearly half an hour on another 12 motions. Some are clerical. One concerns the content of a questionnaire that will be put to potential jurors about how they feel about the death penalty. Another seeks to preclude the presence of electronic media cameras and other devices in the courtroom.

Hutton reminds the judge he wants to enter on the record

facts concerning jury fore*men*. Blackwell relents and Hutton calls to the stand a county clerk's office employee who testifies that no female or African American forepersons have been appointed to the grand juries in Fayette County since 1870.

To prove the population makeup over those thirteen decades, Hutton calls for questioning a University of Memphis librarian. The University's library is a federal depository of various records.

Saundra Williams testifies at length that records show half the population of Fayette County over the time span has been roughly 50 percent female, and that until the 1970s, the majority of people living in the county were African Americans.

Thirty minutes later, with all the numbers aired, Hutton says that he believes a "prima facie" case of racial discrimination has been made. The Latin term means "at first sight" — that is, enough to proceed in law.

"The motion is overruled," Blackwell says.

With that judicial pronouncement, Hutton moves to perhaps the most important motions to be heard in court this long day. The motions are made on behalf of all three defendants and they seek to suppress the statements made by them on the night they were arrested. Defense lawyers intend to indict the very circumstances surrounding their arrests and how the statements were obtained.

In short, did the three young men understand their Constitutional rights? Were they correctly "Mirandized?" Did the defendants "knowingly and intelligently" waive their rights? Were they even competent enough to do so?

The defense teams have pulled out the final implement in their legal tool box.

Now the clock approaches high noon. Blackwell hammers

for a recess until 1 p.m. Some observers hurry to find lunch. Reporters call their offices. Other people loiter in groups outside. Several lawyers compare notes and reset their afternoon strategy.

When court reconvenes after the break, lawyer Massey asks the judge if he may make a brief announcement. It obviously is aimed directly at Bob Lee and his family.

"This is an adversarial system we're in — us lawyers," he begins. "Often times we have obligations imposed upon us by the law and by the courts and it's hard for people who aren't lawyers to understand. But we do care. We are sensitive to the family and to considerations involving them."

Then Massey has a surprise.

"On behalf of Robert Carpenter, right now I say what we are doing is fighting for his life! We withdraw our motion to suppress evidence." No doubt, this is a true statement — that his main objective is to save Carpenter from the death penalty. It's also true that since Antonio's lawyers will proceed with their motion to suppress, Robert's lawyers are simply streamlining the day's proceedings.

Hutton then chimes in: "The only other matter was the doctors are here and they would like to know a date for the mental retardation hearing." Their evidence will shine light, he says, on Robert Carpenter's lack of competence to stand trial.

Simmons stands on behalf of Antonio. "We're ready to proceed with the suppression hearing."

Judge Blackwell sets tentative dates for trials and dismisses Hutton and Massey. Now it is time for Wagerman and Simmons to argue for suppressing key elements of the evidence against Antonio. Over the next 90 minutes they cross-examine Fayette

Sheriff's Investigator Don (Chuck) Pugh, Sheriff's Deputy Ricky Wilson, and Collierville Detective Gannon Hill in a sustained attempt to show that important errors were made in the arrests. The three officers played key roles in the capture and arrests of the defendants.

Pugh is called to the stand first. The prosecution begins the questioning. Assistant D.A. Freeland walks Pugh through a description of the events on June 15 beginning with hearing about the abduction of Ann Lee as Pugh ate lunch in his home on Yager Road, and ending with the capture of Antonio and Eric, the verbal reading of their rights, as well as learning where to find Ann's body.

Wagerman then begins the cross-examination. His questions seek to bring out details of the defendant's condition when he was found hiding in the woods and was arrested. Could he have understood his rights? Was he mishandled or threatened?

Tell me Antonio Carpenter's physical description when you saw him. What was he wearing?

"Jeans and a shirt."

And was he limping in any way?

"I didn't notice anything wrong other than he was profusely sweating."

Was there any blood on him in any location at all that you observed?

"Not that I observed, no, sir."

Did he complain in any way about being injured or hurt in any way at all?

"Not to me."

Did he say anything there when you initially saw him coming up the hill with this other officer?

"No, sir."

He didn't respond to you and you didn't respond to him?

"The only time I spoke to him was, like I said, when we got back to the cars and had separated them and the detective told me that Antonio had something to tell me."

But at that earlier point in time — now, did you know Antonio Carpenter?

"Yes."

So you recognized him when you saw him?

"I live two miles from them and have lived there for 40 years. I know their mama and daddy well."

So you knew who he was?

"Yes."

But you didn't say anything to him initially when you saw him being brought up the hill?

"No, sir. Like I say, Gannon Hill walked up with him. We were occupied with Eric Glover."

Did Antonio Carpenter at that point have handcuffs on him?

"Yes, sir."

And I assume they were cuffed — his hands were cuffed behind his back. Were any other form of restraints placed on him? His legs or his head or anything else?

"Not that I saw."

One set of cuffs behind his back. And it's your testimony he didn't complain in any way about hurting or being injured?

"I did not hear him complain at all."

Wagerman then asks a series of questions to find out how and when Antonio's legal rights were delivered to him. The testimony continues:

Was there an officer in charge of questioning Antonio Carpenter?

"I don't know. Detectives Gannon Hill and Landon Howell were at the car or were together when they walked up and Howell told me that Antonio had something to tell me…. I was kneeling down talking to Eric Glover in the back of a car at that time."

Pugh then is asked more questions about when Antonio's rights were read to him and the circumstances that occurred in the minutes before Antonio decided to give a short statement about where Ann Lee's body could be found.

And to your knowledge was any pressure placed on Antonio Carpenter to give this statement?

"No, sir. I mean, now, I was not with Antonio. You will have to ask the officer that was. But as soon as we got to the cars and they were separated, I stayed with Eric until what I said transpired. What Officer Hill and Office Howell — whether they advised him of his rights again, what questions they asked — I don't know."

Did anyone have their hands on Antonio Carpenter when they were asking him this statement?

"Not that I saw."

Was there anything said to Mr. Carpenter about if he did not talk to you what would happen to him? … Nothing of that kind at all?

"Not that I heard or not that I seen."

Next it is Collierville Detective Gannon Hill's turn to be questioned. Prosecutor Campbell asks the first questions, establishing Hill's part in examining the scene at the Sonic restaurant and then his participation in the chase and arrest.

Campbell got Hill to describe the reading of rights to Antonio and asking whether his captive understood those rights and whether he wished to talk to officers about what happened.

As to the first question, what was his response, if any?

"He said, 'Yes, I do understand.' When I asked him, 'Do you understand these rights?' he said, 'Yes.'"

Was anyone's hand upon him? How were you all situated?

"My hands were upon him. I had him by the arm just as a precaution. He is in custody and we have to maintain that custody."

As to the second question?

"He said, 'No'"

Did he seem dazed, confused or disoriented?

"Not at all."

Upon answering the last two questions, what happened after that?

"At that time, when he said, 'Yes, I wish to make a statement,' I asked him the location of Mrs. Lee… At first he said he didn't know what we were talking about. A few seconds later he did say, 'Well, they said they dropped her off in Marshall County on a back road.'"

Did Mr. Carpenter make any other statements to you?

"Yes. About 10 minutes later he made another statement."

Hill testifies that Antonio told him at this point that Mrs. Lee was behind the house on Yager Road and he believed her to be dead. Now it is Wagerman's turn to examine Hill. He first asks a series of questions, taking Hill back through the arrest of Antonio Carpenter in the woods, the walk back to the cruisers, the reading of his Miranda rights. Thirty three questions and answers later:

Did he appear to be injured in any way as you were walking him back?

"No, sir."

Did you notice any blood on his person?

"I don't believe I did."

Hill testifies that he placed Antonio into a Marshall County, Mississippi squad car and then walked up the hill to his car to call the Collierville Police station to report where he was and what had happened. He said he left Antonio in the car with a Marshall County officer for about 10 minutes.

You don't know what he did to him during the five or 10 minutes you were gone?

"As far as 'did to him' — I mean —"

Well, you said you left to use the phone.

"Yes."

You didn't have eyesight of him the whole time you were gone, did you?

"I could see where the vehicle was, yes...."

But you know when you came back Officer Pannell of the Marshall County Sheriff's Office was talking to him and then what happened?

"That's when — well, I mean, he was talking to him and they yelled up at me."

He's ready to say more?

"He said, 'Gannon, come here. He's got something he wants to tell you.'"

And he told you at that point something different than he'd told you originally?

"That's correct."

What caused him to change his story?

"I don't know. I mean, I can't testify to, you know, something I have no idea about. All I know is they called me down there and said he's got something he wants to tell you."

Now comes a point that all the questioning has been leading to for the past hour.

How long did Officer Pannell talk to him? Did Officer Pannell threaten to "take him down the road?"

"Not that I'm aware of."

Did you hear anybody threaten to" take him down the road" if he didn't talk?

"I never heard anybody threaten him, no."

But you know that Officer Pannell told him something, talked to him?

"Yes."

With that crisp answer, Hill leaves the stand. Now it is Ricky Wilson's turn. First Freeland asks questions allowing Wilson to tell his own part in the chase and capture, and then the interrogations. After about 40 questions, prosecutor Freeland asks if Carpenter appeared to be under the influence of any kind of intoxicant.

"No, sir. He appeared to be eager to talk to me."

Did he have any sort of head injury or any other kind of physical injury which would have caused him pain and make him seek medical treatment?

"Other than being soaking wet?"

That was from what?

"Jumping in the lake. … It was hot that afternoon."

Did you observe any physical abuse administered to Antonio

Carpenter?

"None whatsoever."

Now it is attorney Wagerman's turn. After a series of questions about the arrest and Antonio's placement in a squad car, Wilson's answers parallel what the others had said. In the midst of the cross-examination, Wagerman asks Wilson if he had heard anyone say that they would "take Mr. Antonio Carpenter down the road if he didn't speak?"

"No, sir, not in my presence."

Next Wagerman takes Wilson to the unlikely detail that Antonio told officers who had gone to find Ann Lee's body that the rifle had been thrown about "15 meters" away into the grass.

Now, this 15 meters sounds so unusual. You testified it sounded so unusual... Are you sure that's what he said?

"Yes, sir. It struck me as unusual because most people deal in feet, not meters."

Are you sure that's what he said or did he slur his words?

"He said fifteen meters."

Was the weapon found close to that distance?

"Yes."

Fifteen meters?

"I wasn't on the scene so I can't say exactly how far it was that they found it, but it was close to the body. I believe it was around 40 feet or so."

That brings to a close the strange incident of a drop-out teenager accused of kidnapping and murder and using terminology that surprised everyone. Whether any officer actually suggested — subtly or otherwise — that if Antonio didn't help them find Ann he might be "taken down the road," the idea is left lingering in the stale courtroom air.

What did Bob Lee think of the possibility Antonio had been threatened by one or more officers if he didn't come clean about Ann's whereabouts?

"I don't know. Probably? I don't care. They got the information they needed."

The questions finally wind down. Wilson steps out of the box. Freeland tells the judge that the state has presented proof that the statements were "knowingly and intelligently and voluntarily given and the Miranda rights were read and that the statements oral and written should be admitted."

Blackwood responds, "At this time the statements are admissible" pending any further proof from the defense.

And with that ruling, the long string of motions, the procedural fights and the presentation of proofs and witnesses has ended. A seven-hour day spent in the Somerville courtroom is over.

The defense attorneys are more convinced than ever that their main line of defense — probably their only feasible action — is to fight a penalty of death for the Carpenters.

Lee family members are just as convinced that their wait for justice is far from over.

* * *

New Year's Day 2000 arrives and computer networks everywhere continue working without a hitch. What was known as the "Y2 Scare" and the "Millennium bug" has generated worldwide anxiety. The worries disappear in a poof as calendars turn.

U.S. Attorney General Reno's office announces her decision.

She green-lights a rare federal death penalty for Robert and Antonio Carpenter. Lawyers on both sides of both federal and state cases now know what's at stake.

One can only imagine the conversations that have occurred among the defendants and the defense lawyers. It is early March when the mounting pressure on the brothers brings an unexpected twist in the federal case. Robert's attorneys say he now wants to take a guilty plea. He has turned 20. Antonio, now eighteen, doesn't; he wants a trial to prove his innocence. Prosecutor Arvin insists they must be tried together.

McCalla says he'll issue a ruling on whether there should be separate trials within 10 days.

What the judge learns he faces in that particular period is a judicial inquiry into his own courtroom behavior. Headlines of a different sort will come his way.

Several lawyers have accused McCalla of being verbally abusive. He specifically is cited for a harangue of a defense lawyer during the sentencing of an embezzler. But other courtroom statements made by McCalla also are raised to the Sixth U.S. Judicial Court Council.

McCalla will continue his duties during the investigation that will last more than a year. When a decision is made in August 2001 he will admit to the complaints and issue an apology to lawyers, the bar in general and the judiciary. His punishment will be six months leave and behavioral counseling.

Subsequently, McCalla will rise to chief judge in the U.S. District Court for the Western District of Tennessee. He will build and polish a reputation as one of the nation's most efficient chief judges in the federal system.

Lee has his own succinct opinion of McCalla.

He speaks as the spouse of a victim of a brutal and unthinkable crime as well as someone who has attended every hearing in the case for a year. He has listened ad infinitum to motions, tried to understand petitions and procedures, and taken in every nuance of McCalla's rulings and admonitions.

"I like him!"

Eight

My entire life feels consumed by the case and everything feels out of my control so much of the time.

I get letters and cards — mostly from strangers — nearly every day. Some of them are helpful, some not, but all are well-meaning. I put them aside and re-read the helpful ones from time to time.

Some people suggest books for me to read. They include "When Bad Things Happen To Good People" by Harold Kushner; "Dead Man Walking" by Sister Helen Prejean; "No Time For Goodbyes" by Janice Harris Lord. I find something in each that helps a little. Still, I need something else. I decide to go back to church.

I find, though, that I can't sit still in a pew through the service at St. George's Episcopal Church. I'll start sniffling and have to get up and move about.

One Sunday I begin ushering. It keeps me busy. I don't really hear much that helps in the service, but at least I'm here and I'm searching.

Then comes one particular sermon by Rev. Susan Crawford. It changes my life. Literally, it does.

I know she is talking directly to me. I sit down and I stay seated. It's like there's no one else in the sanctuary. Just her, talking to me.

The sermon is about forgiveness. It comes straight at me and into my heart and it stays there. And from my heart it hits my understanding.

Forgiveness doesn't have to rely on a confession by the guilty parties. It doesn't need the death penalty. It isn't about them. It's about me. I need to forgive to live again.

Of course, taking in this message is just a small first step. The concept of forgiveness can move from my understanding and become just an abstract idea so easily. I am going to have to work at it every day, maybe for the rest of my life. I may wake up one morning with a new, unforgiving thought and then I have to start the process all over again. But I realize that if I don't, they're winning over me too.

This ongoing exercise of learning to forgive will take me places I never thought I'd go. I'll even begin talking to groups of people, making presentations about what happened to Ann, what happened to me and my family.

But know this: I still want to see justice done. I still think the death penalty is right for these men who snuffed out Ann's life for no good reason.

* * *

After all the tedium of hearings and motions, the waiting and boredom, justice begins to click more steadfastly in the month of March, 2000. In fact, to say the legendary Ides of March were approaching would not be a stretch.

In the Roman time of Cicero and Pompey the Great, and of course Julius Caesar, the 15th day of March, known as the Ides of March, was the time to settle debts. Dictator Julius Caesar, paying no attention to the warnings, may have felt he had nothing to worry about, nor any debts to pay. Brutus and his band of assassins felt — and acted — otherwise.

Now, in March 2000, modern judges and juries soon will decide if Antonio and Robert Carpenter, along with Eric Glover, have debts to society they must pay and perhaps pay most dearly.

The case in federal court will become almost anti-climactic for the Lee family and the public. But at the courthouse in Somerville, the need and the calls for justice will be well and graphically on display. Ann's personal loss of freedom and control and her subsequent tortuous and lingering death on hard-packed earth will be nearly indescribable.

Details of the manner of death Ann Lee experienced early in the afternoon of June 15, 1999, begin to come out in hearings well before the first trial. Even for prosecutors, adept at emotional descriptions for juries, it is difficult to find the right words to express the horror and the unprovoked viciousness the three teens are accused of carrying out.

The gross insensitivity and utter meanness of the crime are

beyond words people are accustomed to using. Perhaps U.S. District Attorney Veronica Coleman comes closest at the end of federal proceedings when she characterizes the carjacking and murder in public comments as "one of the most senseless and depraved acts" in her long legal experience.

Depravity is a useful word. It includes the concepts of perversity and wickedness, as coming from a vile and evil spirit of corruption.

One other word helps build an apt picture of why three young men in the year 2000 face the first execution in Tennessee since 1943. That word is "crass." The definitions of crass include these dark concepts: gross, coarse, crude, dense, blatant tastelessness, money grubbing-ness, as well as the demonstration of a total lack of discrimination and sensibility toward another human being.

The word comes to us from the Latin, apparently from another figure in Roman history named Marcus Licinius Crassus. He was said to be the richest of fat cats in the time of Julius Caesar, a man, general, statesman who spun clever plots in the back shadows of Rome to amass even more wealth and power. Crassus was said to be a man without honor or personal rectitude. Contemporary onlookers and later historians agree he exhibited unbounded ambition, greed and cravenness. He was unprincipled, immoral and showed no virtue. He lacked good character and conscientiousness.

Yes, depravity and crassness are words that fit this one particular crime these many centuries later, when one considers the facts about what Ann Lee faced on her final day on earth.

For it was with utmost depraved crassness that the three young men together committed murder that day. Only in state court will the full picture emerge of how they tortured and killed Barbara Ann Lee for her second-hand SUV and for her money and to ensure her silence.

The person who will best draw that picture is the man who is most familiar with the results of her ordeal: Shelby County Medical Examiner Dr. O.C. Smith.

In his written autopsy report and on the witness stand in Somerville, Smith lays out the cruel facts.

Ann Lee "died as a result of blows to the head, crushing neck injuries, crushed chest, crushed abdomen and pelvis." He calls her injuries "massive." Ann Lee had tire tracks visible on the left side of her rib cage. He says she also sustained "blunt trauma to the head," an injury consistent with being hit in the head with a rifle stock.

The blow to her skull wasn't sufficient to cause her death, he says. After she was hit and fell to the ground, she remained alive, probably for at least several minutes, as the attack continued. Smith finds that she had sustained multiple blows to her face and deep bruises to her left arm. He says "a fair amount of force was applied to the inside of the left arm for some purpose."

Additionally there was some form of "crushing forces" to the front of her neck, causing a severe case of neck compression. This meant that her voice box, trachea and larynx all were crushed. Smith says these injuries were consistent with a round object — such as a rifle barrel — being pushed with force against her neck. He also surmises that it was probable she had been jumped on at some point during her ordeal.

Smith testifies Ann Lee was alive when she received the crushing force to the neck, she was alive when she received thirty-eight rib fractures, and she was alive when her pelvis was smashed and when her abdomen was crushed.

He determines that the crushing of her torso and abdomen was the direct result of "slow injuries" by a vehicle. He says that means that the car was not moving at a high speed when it rolled over her more than once.

"It's possible," he testifies, "that she was either moving under the vehicle — either being moved by the vehicle or she was moving herself; that the injuries to the back side would indicate that we've got injuries going in one direction, but the injury pattern to the front of her chest indicates another direction." The SUV was driven forward and backward over the dying Ann.

Smith says he couldn't determine for certain whether she was conscious still when she was run over repeatedly by her own vehicle — perhaps moving or even trying to crawl away — many minutes after the attack began.

Smith's testimony — it would prove critical in the state trials — then moves to his finding that torture was involved in the slaying. Smith is introduced in court — and again in the later appeals process — as an expert in the subspecialty of torture in forensic pathology. He says in court that a killing amounts to torture if it involves the concepts of dependency, degradation and dread.

"The dependency is evidenced in the fact that total control has been placed over the victim in her own vehicle and then she's taken away from her normal surroundings and put in an area that is totally controlled by the people who conducted her there.

"Evidence of the psychological depression that goes with degradation is the realization she had; the comment she made that

'You are going to kill me, aren't you?'"

There is further degradation when family photos are removed from her wallet and degrading comments are made, Smith says.

"The dread is seen where she realizes that she will probably not survive the incident," Smith goes on. "As a component of dread, execution (comes) through the severe physical abuse, rapid physical assault in which a person may fear for life or limb."

When Smith's report and testimony are read side-by-side against the statements made by the Carpenters and Glover the night of their arrests — even though they point fingers at each other and never clear up discrepancies — it is possible to discern the probable sequence and the physical blows in a cruel, depraved — utterly crass — attack that led finally to her death.

It is all too easy to visualize Ann Lee's last minutes in life. Only the sounds of birdcalls, a panting Schnauzer and the whisper of wind in the trees are in the background.

When the vehicle comes to a stop in the woods Ann is told to get out. She probably knows she is taking her final breaths. As she faces away, and after begging that her dog not be harmed, the wooden rifle butt is swung against the back of her skull.

She falls down, stunned, but tries to move away. She either turns over or someone turns her face-up. The rifle is then held against her throat by at least two hands. Other hands may grab and hold her arms in place as she struggles.

She doesn't yet die. She is in agony.

It then seems probable that one or more people jump on her upper chest, perhaps repeatedly. Even still, she is alive, but mercifully she may be losing consciousness.

Now she is left to die alone, but only for as long as it takes for the Blazer to be driven the three-quarters of a mile to and from the house where the murderous trio learn police officers have come by.

Robert Carpenter drives the stolen vehicle back to the killing place where the Blazer runs over Ann Lee's body, forward and backward, at least twice. This crushes her ribcage, abdomen and pelvis. The men get out and drag her body to a ditch. They cover her with branches and rugs, hiding her body, her face, her eyes. Now, most likely, she is dead.

Her purse is emptied, credit cards and other belongings are scattered in the weeds. Two of the men change into the Eddie Bauer clothes Ann purchased two hours before for husband Bob.

The sawed-off rifle that never had any bullets is tossed "fifteen meters" or about 50 feet away in ankle-high grass.

And Ann's loyal dog is tied to an old wire fence.

Otis knows what happened. He can't talk. That's probably why he wasn't killed, too.

NINE

We finally are approaching the trials. I am filled inside with turmoil. There could be many days, weeks in courtrooms. There could be relief, or there could be unbelievable tension. And I still am trying to truly forgive these men I've considered monsters. I realize more and more that forgiving others really is about yourself more than it about those who hurt you. It doesn't make any difference if they accept your forgiveness.

That's hard, hard stuff, let me tell you. Forgiving — the decision itself — takes you away from what's happening so you can put it elsewhere deep inside. For me that means in God's hands.

I soon learn it's not a straight or sequential path that you take. There have been weeks at a time where I've fallen back in the same old groove of hating. Every time I have to climb back out of that familiar but dark mental and emotional hole. My kids give me three good reasons to keep at it. I couldn't be much of a father or grandfather if I am forever dwelling in anger, with the overwhelming need to get even.

This mental process — forgiving three murderers — is taking all year and will probably take even longer.

During the first hearings I wanted to shoot them. Kill them. But when the first trial comes along, something clicks inside. I pretty much want them to get the most punishment they can, but most of the time I don't want them to get the death penalty any more. I don't want to say that publicly, you understand. I still worry about what people would think. Yet, I know their executions wouldn't fix anything. And I'd have to live with this for years as the appeals roll on. I just have to put it all in God's hands — especially whether they should live or die.

And here's the thing — the longer I can stay in that mode of thinking, the better off I am. Don't get me wrong. It's not like turning a light switch: Snap! Forgiveness! I'm all better now!

During this dragging out time there is one thing I sometimes want to know. Then I don't want to know. Or — yes, I do. Who did what to Ann and who didn't do it, but didn't stop it either?

This was like another light switch in me.

One that might take years to flip.

* * *

For everything under heaven there is a season, so the book of Ecclesiastes says, and in early spring of 2000 the season finally arrives for trying Eric Glover and Robert and Anthony Carpenter

Eric Glover at trial.

in courts of law. It has been more than nine months since the crime. The Lee family has somehow lived, endured, stumbled through summer, fall and winter. Now they are in the time of Lent on the Christian liturgical calendar, a time of preparation for the Resurrection, a time for life anew during the lengthening of days.

The opening trial will be for Glover, the youngest of the accused. He does not face execution. The strongest punishment that can come his way is life in prison without the possibility of a parole. The proceedings begin in Fayette County on a cool Monday morning, March 21, 2000.

It is indeed the first full day of spring.

The defendant, neatly-dressed and wearing glasses, is escorted in by Sheriff's deputies under the steady gaze of Bob and his daughter Liz. Minutes later the trial begins. The prosecutors are Assistant District Attorneys Colin Campbell and Walt Freeland. Defense attorney Shana McCoy-Johnson stands next to Glover as the room is called to order. No evidence is brought forth that hasn't already been heard in court and published in the press. The only question argued by the lawyers is the extent of Glover's "responsibility" for Ann Lee's death. He doesn't appear on the stand. The jury is sequestered for the night.

On Tuesday, the trial moves swiftly to closing arguments.

"Imagine what was going on in Barbara Ann Lee's mind on that one-way road to death," Campbell says, peering at each juror. Glover's guilt in the crime is no less certain under the law than that of a get-away driver in a robbery, Freeland adds when it's his turn.

Don't judge him on the basis of what others may have done, McCoy-Johnson says when she sums up for the defense. Find him

115

guilty only for what he did.

It is an interesting suggestion when one considers it has been so far impossible to know exactly who did what to Ann Lee. Glover, at least, apparently believes there is plenty of doubt sown about the extent of his participation.

The jury takes just over an hour to reach a verdict of guilty on four counts of aggravated murder and kidnapping. "Damn," a stunned Glover says aloud as he hears the first verdict read by the foreman.

"As if in shock the teenager placed both his hands over his head," reports Lela Garlington in the next day's *The Commercial Appeal*. "As the foreman continued with three additional counts of guilty Glover's mouth dropped open. He stared at the jury in disbelief."

The sentencing phase of the trial starts after a short break. Glover takes the stand and speaks words of remorse. Liz Lee again supplies an impact statement on behalf of the family. Her main theme is that victims and their families don't seem to get the same rights or attention as do the accused, and her words sear:

"Maybe it's time the judges and attorneys really listen to the victims' families. Hear all of the pain we are going through. Listen to what we want. Because it's our family who has suffered the loss of a loved one.

"We are the ones who will miss her every day. We are the ones who will re-live the pain every time there is an appeal."

This time the jury of seven men and five women needs just three quarters of an hour to choose his punishment: a life sentence. He must spend 51 years in prison before he will be eligible to be paroled. He'll be sixty-eight. His youthfulness— and some doubts as to his exact role in the murder — are mentioned afterwards by jurors as extenuating circumstances. They say only one juror argued for a life sentence without any chance of parole.

During the trial, Bob Lee takes time as usual to speak to reporters. The see-saw of his thoughts and emotions is evident.

"My evil side says, 'Fry him,'" he tells them plainly. "Mainly, I hope he can come to terms with what he did..."

One trial is suddenly over, but there's little time to ponder the outcome because in less than a week, the Carpenter brothers' federal trial is scheduled to begin and plenty of drama seems set for the U.S. Courthouse in downtown Memphis.

* * *

A preliminary hearing for the two men is held two days after Glover's trial ends. U.S. Judge McCalla listens to arguments for and against having one trial for the two Carpenters. Defending lawyers argue for separate trials. Prosecutors want one trial. The hearing goes an hour. McCalla rules that the prosecution can have one trial but says he will instruct the jury to consider the evidence against each defendant separately. The judge also turns down defense lawyer Howard Wagerman's request for a sequestered jury, saying he'll keep an open mind as proceedings take place.

One day after the hearing, a federal panel begins its inquiry into McCalla's courtroom behavior. The investigation will continue concurrent with the Carpenters' trial and beyond.

Assistant U.S. Attorney Tony Arvin explains his trial tactics to Bob.

"He said he expected neither one would be inclined to tell the same story," Bob recalls years later. "That's why he wanted to try the two together. It would make it harder for them to point a finger at each other if they were sitting there next to each other on trial."

Robert Carpenter now wants to take a plea agreement for life in prison in order to get out from under the death penalty. His brother says he wants a trial. Unless both ask for a plea agreement, a single trial will happen the following week. Jury selection is set to begin on Monday.

That day the jury selection opens and moves at a snail's pace. Bob Lee stays home on the advice that the proceedings will be tedious. Once a jury is in place, the trial is expected to go two weeks or longer.

A large pool of prospective jurors gradually diminishes because of medical or scheduling problems or because of what individuals say about how they feel about the death penalty. One woman says she's been trying to come to grips with what she thinks of the penalty all her life and still isn't sure. She is dismissed. Court adjourns in the afternoon and resumes the next morning. By the end of the second day, there seem to be enough jurors, depending on how many are struck by attorneys.

Each side can strike up to 20. The prosecution says it needs five minutes to decide whom to strike. The defense lawyers say they'll need about an hour.

But a flurry of activity late in the day tells savvy court onlookers that something might be happening in the background. Lawyers begin going in and out a courtroom door leading to a room where the brothers wait.

In ongoing discussions all week among the brothers, their lawyers and various family members, attempts have been made to convince Antonio Carpenter to plead guilty.

On Wednesday morning the question of striking potential

jurors indeed is forgotten as it is announced that both brothers now want to enter plea agreements with the government. There will be no trial and no federally-ordered execution. The duo will get life in prison without a possibility of parole for Ann's murder.

At least, Bob says, he and his family "won't have to go through the rigors" of federal death penalty appeals.

* * *

On May 29, 2000 — a warming Wednesday afternoon — the brothers stand in front of Judge McCalla's high bench. Behind them are eight attorneys. Several U.S. marshals form an outer ring.

Pleading guilty in this case is not a brief undertaking. Court Reporter Lynn Dudley types 83 pages for the official record of the *United States of America, Plaintiff, vs. Robert Lewis Carpenter, Jr. and Antonio Dewayne Carpenter, Defendants.*

The two men are about to confess for the first time officially in court to kidnapping and murdering Barbara Ann Lee.

Judge McCalla takes his good time. He is deferential, almost charming. Before the defendants are brought into the courtroom McCalla learns from defense lawyers that the men want to plead guilty to the federal charges.

"Now, gentlemen," the judge says, "We are going to have them both brought in, and I know that you just finished talking to them a second ago and you're just making the announcement and the marshals will stand up here, and I'm going to have one a little bit on one side and one on the other. Naturally, that is how we always do this."

A U.S. marshal approaches the bench to confer on a request by the defendants.

"You all go ahead and we'll get situated," McCalla replies.

"They'll have three or four minutes to smoke their cigarettes and come on in here, all right?

"Judge, we're going in … just one moment we'll be ready," Arvin says.

"Oh, no, that's fine," McCalla responds. I want you to take the time you need, gentlemen… Let's take about five minutes, and I'm going to be up here organizing my papers for this."

Judge McCalla is demonstrating the very model of judicial behavior and deference. When things start back several minutes later, the brothers stand before the bench. They are wearing suits and their shoes are shined.

"Feeling a little better?" he asks Robert Carpenter.

"Yes," the defendant replies.

"Come a little bit forward and speak into that microphone so I can hear you real well, okay? Mr. Antonio Carpenter, how are you today?

"I'm all right," the younger Carpenter says.

McCalla then has the court clerk perform a swearing-in of the two. After that the judge asks a series of questions with the purpose of identifying them by name, birth, education and work experiences, medical history and their ability to read.

His questions are specific. Robert's answers mostly consist of one, two or three words. Antonio elaborates a little more and is more polite. Both slouch a bit.

McCalla asks the two about the decision they are making in court this day. His long line of inquiries is meant to demonstrate the two understand what is happening and are pleading guilty of their own free will. He first questions Robert.

And would you tell us who you've talked with in this case

Robert and Anthony Carpenter at a preliminary hearing.

about the decision that you were going to make today?

"The lawyers."

The lawyers. What about your aunt?

"Yeah, my aunt."

Did you talk with your brother at all about it?

"Yeah."

All right. Did you talk to anybody else about it?

"No."

All right. Well, now are they making you plead guilty?

"No."

Why are you going to plead guilty then?

"The right thing to do."

All right. Did you make up your own mind about that?

"Yes."

Has that been something that you have been thinking about for a long time?

"Yes."

And have you thought that you maybe ought to do that for months now, is that right or wrong? I don't know — January, February? This is March.

"Yeah"

How many months have you been thinking about that?

"January."

Since January. In fact, I understand that perhaps you were willing to plead guilty back in January if you could bring this case to a conclusion, is that right?

"Yes."

(A lawyer interjects. "I believe when the Court asked earlier about who he had spoken with and the Court knew he had spoken with more people than what he said — that's who he has spoken with today …")

And in the past you may have spoken to some other people . . .?

"Yes."

And some other relatives? Your mother, did you talk to her?

"Yes."

Which brother did you talk to?

"All of them."

Really? All of them. … now, let me ask you this: have these people been trying to force you to plead guilty in any way?

"No."

You told me that you'd been treated for some mental conditions ... are you taking any medicine now?

"I was at the time but not at the present."

And do you know what that medicine was for?

"Naw."

(Lawyer interjects: Your Honor, I think he's been treated numerous times over the years. I would point out his IQ is 60 to 70, Your Honor.)

I realize that. I realize. And that's why we're having this conversation.

McCalla finds out from Robert that he has been addicted to marijuana and cigarettes and that he is at that moment having pain in his knee.

Is that affecting your understanding of what we're doing today?

"Naw."

McCalla then addresses Antonio.

I know the lawyer has been speaking for you before, but I'm going to have to hear from you in this matter. Is that okay?

"Yes."

Did you have any activities that you participated in while you were in school ...?

"A little basketball, sir."

Some basketball. You ever been addicted to drugs of any kind?

"Yes."

And what drugs would those be? A little bit ... some

marijuana.

"Yeah."

Did you use it every day?

"No."

How often?

"Special occasions."

Special occasions, all right. Do you smoke cigarettes?

"Yes."

Okay. You drink alcohol?

"Yes."

Beer sometimes?

"Naw. I don't drink beer."

What would you drink?

"Liquor."

Now, I'm going to ask you this: are you currently under the influence of anything? Any drugs or alcohol, medication, anything at all?

"Well, I took a little medication but, you know, it ain't no strong medication you know."

What was it for?

"For depression."

Do you know what the medicine was?

"Zoloft."

Does that help with your depression?

"Yes."

Well, is that making you make a decision or are you able to do this on your own?

"Made me do it on my own."

McCalla then moves Antonio toward the specific charges and

whether he has been satisfied with his attorneys (Wagerman and Simmons).

"Of course."

Have they been putting pressure on you to change your plea or is this something you want to do?

"Something I want to do."

Now, who else did you talk to about making this decision?

"My aunty."

Your aunt?

"My lawyer."

What about your brothers?

"This marshal here, sir."

The marshal?

"My Momma and the Lord, sir."

All right. And have any of them made any threat to you or tried to make you plead guilty in this case?

"No."

Is this your decision? Is this what you want to do?

"Yes, sir."

Plead guilty?

"Yes."

And why do you want to do it?

"Well, I feel by the law I'm guilty to the charges brought against me."

McCalla then turns to Robert to ask whether his lawyers have done right by him and whether he has reviewed the charges. The answers are in the affirmative.

The next hour of the hearing is a confirmation of the charges and the pleadings. Asst. U.S. Attorney Arvin explains they are pleading guilty to all three counts of the federal indictment, they do so willingly and without coercion and that in exchange for the pleas the government "will not seek the death penalty; we will waive the death penalty and recommend that they be sentenced to life imprisonment … they will not be paroled from their life sentence; there is no parole in the federal system…

"And further, Your Honor, the defense counsel have stipulated, and we would — and we would ask that the record reflect that both defendants have been examined by defense-hired psychologists and/or psychiatrists and found competent, mentally competent to stand trial and/or plead guilty."

McCalla now wants to make certain the two men realize they will live out their lives in prison.

Mr. Robert Carpenter, do you understand that?
"Yes."
And how long do you understand that you will be in prison?
"The rest of my natural life."
Mr. Antonio Carpenter, do you understand that?
"Yes."
How long do you understand you will be in prison?
"The rest of my life."

The judge isn't finished. An aunt of the two has come to Memphis from Georgia. And he asks if she is satisfied the two know what they face. She says they do.

Then McCalla tells the two what civil rights they are giving up — voting, serving on a jury, possessing a firearm, holding public office — and "to ever have any freedoms at all in terms of being outside of prison."

Do you understand that you are giving all of that up?

(Antonio responds first.) "Well, I understand I'm giving up my freedom, but them other things, Your Honor, I didn't plan to do too many of them anyway."

Mr. Robert Carpenter, you understand you are giving all of that up?

"Yes."

To further ensure there are no doubts, McCalla questions the pair on each count in the indictment and whether they absolutely understand what penalty each carries. Each count carries a $250,000 fine as well as life in prison. "But I understand — we don't have money here, obviously."

The Judge now has taken everyone about half way through the day's proceedings. He next explains their rights to a trial by jury in detail and asks questions to ascertain that they understand what trial rights they are giving up by pleading guilty. They both say they do.

McCalla walks them through each count and how each specifically pertains to the abduction and death of Ann and that their intent was to cause death or serious bodily injury, and that in each case their guilt would have to be proved by prosecutors.

Again and again and again Robert and Antonio Carpenter respond with repeated yeses and yeahs.

Still, Judge McCalla isn't finished. He then invites Arvin to tell the charges against the two. Arvin narrates what he would have proved in court. He begins his account with Ann Lee driving into Slot 22 at the Collierville Sonic restaurant and her kidnapping at gunpoint, tells of the search for the Blazer, the chase into Mississippi, the capture of three suspects, police officers finding Ann's body at the end of the dirt road, and the extent of her fatal injuries.

Defense attorneys then stipulate that those are the essential facts of the case.

The Carpenters are asked how they plead on each of the counts. "Guilty," both reply three times.

There remains only the need for McCalla to adjudge them guilty and to say for the record that lawyers on both sides worked in good faith, were governed by the rules of law and that fairness was upheld.

One last time, he asks the defendants if they feel their rights had always been protected throughout the proceedings. Both reply that they did.

It is after 4 p.m. McCalla has left nothing to chance. In a reading of the transcript of the hearing, one can only believe that the Carpenters were entering their guilty pleas with full knowledge and understanding of what they were admitting and what their admissions meant to them personally.

That, however, won't keep them from appealing later on the grounds that they did not fully comprehend what their guilty pleas meant.

Judge McCalla sets a date in June for sentencing. His only duty remaining this day is to call in the jurors, who are standing by in case something interrupts the pleas, to dismiss them from their civic service.

* * *

The Lee family receives nearly a month's reprieve from attending court sessions. They next will travel back to Somerville where the Carpenter brothers still face the death penalty in their State of Tennessee trials. This springtime holds more unexpected drama, beginning with a hearing in April.

Judge Blackwood is ready to consider a motion filed by Robert Carpenter's defense attorneys — Robert Hutton and William Massey —that he be ruled mentally retarded and therefore ineligible to be put to death by the state. The attorneys bring in two expert witnesses from Vanderbilt University in Nashville who testify that Robert scores in the mid-sixties on tests, showing he has mild mental retardation. The testimony accompanies documents entered into the record detailing the man's home and school experiences and psychological examinations over several years.

The documents amount to a dossier on Carpenter and his family. The material reads like a multi-year rundown of what is surely a terrible childhood, but also myriad attempts by educators, social workers and psychologists to save a troubled juvenile from anti-social behavior and self-destruction. Some information had been made public in a state hearing the previous summer.

Robert grew up with fifteen brothers and sisters in poverty, living part of the time at home and part of the time in foster care. He had witnessed a shooting before he was 10. He said he was burned with lighter fluid by his father for punishment, something Robert Carpenter, Sr. denied.

As he reached his teens, he was constantly in trouble in school. By the time he was 15 years old he had stolen his first car and attempted suicide more than once.

In September, 1995, he was admitted to an emergency room after trying to hang himself at the Shelby County Training Center. A psychiatric evaluation at the time gave a harrowing account of his life:

"Robert reports onset of hearing voices at age eight or nine. He reports severe insomnia due to voices at night telling him to kill himself. He is psychotically depressed ... he reports frequently hearing command hallucinations to kill himself or hurt others ..."

The psychiatrist listed multiple special behavioral problems, including suicidal tendencies, assaults, fire-setting, substance abuse, theft and attempts to run away. The report then said the "patient witnessed his mother shoot his uncle; witnessed his mother having sex on several occasions with multiple partners; witnessed cocaine and heroin use" and more.

The month before the report was made Carpenter had been placed in the custody of the Shelby Youth Bureau after having run away from the educational training center where he was enrolled, and stolen a Jeep. In January of 1996 he admits to having stolen ten or twelve vehicles before getting caught.

All these facts make up one page of a 42-page document on his childhood troubles.

By the end of the hearing Blackwood has heard and read enough about Robert Carpenter's life. He rules in favor of the defense motion. The man cannot be put to death under Tennessee authority for the killing of Ann Lee. He still can be tried for her murder, however.

By now the Lee family has stopped demanding the death penalty. They want an assurance that the brothers will be kept in prison their entire lives with no chance of living free. With long months of judicial system experience behind them, the Lees believe they understand how things work. But they are in for a new surprise, and so is Judge Blackwood.

On Tuesday May 16, Antonio Carpenter astounds the judge

and his own attorneys when he stands before the bench and turns down two offers that would save him from a potential execution. Wearing chains at his ankles and wrists, he is taller than a year ago and now sports a small mustache. He walks stiffly into the Fayette County Courthouse, guarded by deputies on each side, and watched by Bob Lee and his daughters Liz and Dorene.

The prosecutors and defense attorneys have come up with two ways forward that would save Carpenter from a possible death sentence. He has been offered life without parole if he will plead guilty. He also has been offered life without parole if he will assent to a non-jury trial. He bluntly refuses both offers.

Blackwood peers through his round glasses at Carpenter's attorneys.

"It's our position this is suicide, Your Honor," says attorney James Simmons.

Blackwood turns to Antonio Carpenter, who has set his face in a look of stubbornness and defiance. The judge, wagging his finger, questions him thoroughly. Does Carpenter realize he already is set for three life sentences and no chance of parole in federal court? Does he understand the State of Tennessee is willing to give up the penalty of death? Does he further realize that in a trial by jury the chance of the death penalty remains? Does he perceive that the jury during trial may be told of his guilty plea in federal court? That means there will be no question of your guilt, the judge explains.

"Do you understand all that? And, let me tell you something else," Blackwood says sternly. "If we bring a jury in here to try this case, there's no backing out."

Blackwood also tells Antonio that if he thinks during a trial

131

he might have an opportunity to escape, he will not have any such opportunity.

"I understand," Antonio replies more than once. "I don't want it (the prosecution's offers)."

After the hearing, Antonio's second attorney, Howard Wagerman, obviously exasperated, tells reporters, "There is no rational explanation for his decision."

But it seems everyone at the courthouse has a theory: he's not smart enough to see what lies before him; he thinks he's being crafty; he'll give in in the end, just before a trial will begin, and he really does hope he can somehow escape several guards one day when transferred from jail to court and back again, even while shackled. After all, the brothers came close to escaping once before.

Another possibility exists.

Antonio might think he has some control over what is happening and will happen to him by refusing his attorneys' advice and saying no to the man wearing a black robe. In court every eye is on him. Everyone listens to whatever he has to say. Perhaps, in his mind, being in court is better than being in a jail cell.

He also might believe, as apparently Eric Glover believed, that people ultimately will understand that it was his brother who was in charge the fateful June day in 1999. Robert was the leader, wasn't he?

Doesn't that make Antonio himself less guilty somehow?

But soon facts will surface showing that Antonio Carpenter indeed has been plotting a way to obtain his freedom.

In prison during the winter, the younger brother wrote at least

two letters — in printed characters and on lined pages —
containing an elaborate plan. He urged Robert to claim that
Antonio had nothing to do with the kidnapping and killing of Ann
Lee. Once free, Antonio promised to help his brother escape
prison.

"Get those answers together in your head," the letter said.

"I was not at that Sonic. Tell them I didn't know where that
money came from you gave me. Or I didn't drive that Blazer. I
think that's it. Oh, and I didn't choke that woman…

"You lay low for about a month…. I'm coming to get you."

He added in the letters that his brother should tear them up
after reading. Robert handed them over to his lawyers instead and
they turned them in to prosecutors.

Authorities now figure Antonio will attempt to escape on his
own. The Fayette County Sheriff's Office makes plans to tighten
security.

* * *

Temperatures in Memphis and Somerville flirt with the 90s
as June of 2000 arrives. The end of the trials finally is in sight.
Judge Jon McCalla has set sentencing for Tuesday, June 6. The
brothers haven't seen each other since March. They sit in their
chairs with poker faces, looking away from each other as court is
brought to order.

McCalla first delivers the three life-without-parole sentences
to Robert, who stands with his attorneys. When it is his turn,
Antonio slouches further in his chair and refuses to stand. Lawyers
and U.S. marshals stand up around him as McCalla reads his fate
into the record.

McCalla notes that pre-sentencing reports recommend that

the brothers not serve time in the same Tennessee prison, and that ends the short sentencing hearing. The pair is loaded into separate vehicles for the drive back to incarceration at a Nashville prison, but soon they will be driven west again for trials in Fayette County.

The first — for Robert Carpenter — opens June 15. Exactly one year ago he, his brother and Eric Glover had carjacked, tortured and killed Ann Lee.

The trial is fairly brief. A little after 1:30 in the afternoon — the very time the crime at the Collierville Sonic restaurant had started — Judge Blackwood sentences Robert to prison for the rest of his life. For the Lee family, part of a long ordeal seems to be coming to a close. Bob gives quotes to reporters in a hallway.

Then a deputy approaches. Robert Carpenter wants to speak with Bob.

"I thought he wanted to apologize," Bob said later. "Maybe show some remorse. But he really wanted to minimize his part. Blame the others."

Even so, part of what Robert says gives a little more detail of Ann's final moments, if the man can be believed.

"God, forgive me my sins. I'm dying." Those were among Ann's final words, says the convicted killer.

The brief encounter leaves Bob dissatisfied, but he is glad the man made some kind of attempt. "Maybe that in itself is some kind of remorse," Bob surmises.

One more month must go by before it is Antonio's time to face a jury. First, on July 17, Blackwood holds a hearing to determine his competency. Witnesses appear for both sides. The witnesses for the prosecution have made their case, says

Blackwood: Antonio is competent to stand trial. Two days later the actual trial begins.

Summer thunderstorms are rolling through West Tennessee.

Plenty of guards are on hand to prevent any mischief, such as an escape attempt. The trial doesn't take long. Shelby County Medical Examiner O.C. Smith explains the extent of Ann's fatal injuries and how her murder amounts to torture.

Attorney Marty McAfee speaks in Antonio's defense. The accused has long since given up on his other lawyers. McAfee puts all the blame on brother Robert.

"Am I here to tell you that what he did was admirable?" he asks the jury.

Lightning and thunder boom outside the court. Rain pelts the windows. The lights even flicker.

"No. Perhaps he should have done more to prevent this from happening. But it was Robert who had the gun, drove the Blazer and killed her. There's no way to explain why Antonio Carpenter and Eric Glover could not talk him out of it."

That was the essence of the defense.

Annie Benton, Antonio and Robert's mother, is on the witness list. She had agreed to speak on her son's behalf. When the time comes, she doesn't answer a deputy's call. She has failed to show up for her son.

The jury finds Antonio guilty as charged. The next day the panel deliberates for an hour. The 12 panelists decide against the death penalty because of mitigating circumstances — childhood neglect and abuse.

Bob's son Robert, Jr. has driven from Birmingham to join his family. He finds the jury's mercy hard to take and says so to reporters.

"If a crime as heinous as that doesn't deserve the death penalty I don't know what does," he says. His father adds that he hopes "maybe some other kids won't try to do the same thing. Maybe they'll stop and think, 'Hey, the Carpenter boys got put away forever.'"

Bob takes time over the next few days to consider further the jury's verdict. He writes his thoughts in a letter to the editor of *The Commercial Appeal*. His letter concludes that what the jury ruled, in so many words, was this: "It's a real bad thing those boys did, but not *that* bad."

TEN

The trials are over and all I can think is, "What do I do now?"

I'm alone at home with Otis and our cat Dixie when I return each day from work. No TV crews meet me at the door. Nobody is calling for interviews. No more casseroles from neighbors and strangers with kindness in their hearts.

Cooking is a chore. Usually I just pour a bowl of cereal. I try to eat out but sitting alone in a restaurant is no fun, believe me. It seems to me everyone is looking at me. I feel lost. I know Ann's murder and the aftermath define me now. I want that to change.

Otis has what must be separation anxiety and I can't cope with it. My daughter Dorene offers to take him. We meet at a midway point between Memphis and Nashville for the transfer. I cry most of the drive home.

This fight within me to forgive Ann's killers often doesn't seem to be working. My sorrow grows each day. I know I'm finally grieving. But I hate the Carpenter brothers and Eric. I just really hate them and I want to even the score. I have nightmares about the three and my longing for revenge. At church I talk with another parishioner whose wife died. He has remarried. He tells me to move on. I think about dating but that scares me after 40 years. And what would the children think?

Because of several months' loss of salary, I'm so far behind on my mortgage that foreclosure looms. I sell the house and it's just enough to pay the arrears on the place. I'm embarrassed about that.

I find an apartment. Dorene and her friends help me move. In the apartment I begin to recall all the details of my life with Ann, beginning with a double date. I remember so much as if it happened yesterday. She goes out with my Navy buddy and my date is her friend. I talk over my keen interest in Ann later with my friend and he says, "Go for it."

Barbara Ann Lyons is the fifth and last child of Otto and Mary Lyons. Her growing-up life in Memphis suburbs centers on animals, especially horses. She is an accomplished rider. After we marry the Navy transfers me to Georgia. We move a lot, living in Memphis, Minnesota, back to Memphis, Birmingham, Mobile, Memphis again, then Wisconsin. We finally return to Memphis and Ann resumes her life with horses. She trains and breeds horses and teaches riding skills. All that and more I relive in my mind.

Flying airplanes has long been a hobby. One day a friend at the airport asks me to help another friend who is having a problem with her computer. It takes me a long while — several visits — to fix that computer. She too likes flying. We start meeting at the airport. After several months, I fall in love again with this woman named Mary. Her support is crucial to being able to forgive. Something powerful happens inside me. Forgiveness is no longer a painful abstract concept that I'd rather not think about. It's real now and something— anger and hatred, I know — is dissolving slowly.

I feel it happening. My God, I really do,

* * *

Now and then comes a period of time in a person's life that is so filled with events and emotions that they can't be experienced truly, fully in the present — the moments, days, even months that they happen. That is Bob Lee's life from June 15, 1999 until July 20, 2000 when the last trial is finished.

Thirteen months of living hell has reached some kind of pause. Sitting on hard benches in various courtrooms isn't completely behind him, but Bob finds time to think and take stock and to go over everything in his mind since Ann Lee met death at road's end.

Can there now, somehow, be life after death at road's end?

Gradually he begins to think that is possible. He knows to expect appeals of the convictions. They will be filed and heard and the sentences quickly upheld by state and federal appeals courts over the next 15 months. Meantime Bob has a chance to get his life in order. It helps that he has returned to work where he can dive into computers and networks all day long. He returns to his love of flying small-engine planes on weekends and later will resume his hobby of building hardwood furniture.

Still, money woes weigh on him.

"I was getting low on funds," he recalls later, sitting behind his desk in a new home. "I sold the house but got nothing to help with going forward."

One potential route out of those difficulties is promising, though — a civil lawsuit he filed months before against the Sonic Restaurants national company and local franchise holders.

"I went to see a friend after a lady called and said I should check my insurance carrier to see if there might be funds available since Ann's murderers were uninsured drivers. I asked him about that. He told me, 'No, you can't get anywhere with that. But I know an attorney who used to work with us on insurance cases. His name's Gary Smith. Go see him.'"

Bob calls the next morning and meets with Smith who tells him he indeed has a case he can pursue.

"I at first saw it, honestly, as another way to satisfy my need to get revenge. After all, they were involved. I never felt good about the restaurant allowing the conditions that made it possible for the carjacking. Gary convinces me there is a strong case and so I agree."

The suit is filed. Over a period of several months depositions are taken and a private investigator interviews employees, employees' friends, and two of the convicted men in prison. Information slowly comes to light indicating that to varying degrees several people knew of the Carpenters' plans to carjack somebody. Some even believed they were serious. One employee helped them obtain an old sawed-off rifle from north Mississippi, the very weapon used in the abduction and killing.

All the incriminating facts ultimately will prompt a settleement offer in the six-figure range. Bob, weary of courtrooms and legal fights, takes the offer. He feels the settlement is enough to help him get his life back on track.

Money, of course, may pay the bills but isn't a magic elixir. Susan Gillpatrick, the social worker who helped Bob through the court hearings, suggests that he tell his experiences publicly to church groups, clubs and other organizations, especially groups of victims and the families of victims. Bob does and it gives him a new purpose in life. He joins a taskforce advising the mayor of Shelby County on ways to meet the needs of victims of crime. He becomes one of its strongest voices. His presence adds a dignity and a reality to the work of the group.[iv]

Bob senses he has a future. Mary makes that a concrete concept.

Even so, Bob Lee's thoughts often linger over unresolved facts. He harbors what he considers a reasonable expectation that one or more of the three killers may at some point feel — and even express — some real degree of remorse for what they did.

Maybe not contrition. But surely some form of regret or sorrow — some showing of self-reproach beyond that exhibited by the youngest, Eric Glover, during the sentencing phase of his trial.

"Of course, that might not be true remorse," Bob muses to himself at one point. "That might be self-pity that he had been found guilty and received a long sentence."

He often imagines— he knows it is just a daydream — visiting the trio in prison and hearing words of penance. In his vision, they beg for forgiveness. They plead, hands outstretched.

He watches for any opportunity for a real meeting and one

finally comes.

During the early phase of his civil case, Bob's attorneys had hired a private investigator to gather facts about the defendants, some Sonic employees and people in their circles.

In early 2003 the sleuth's work takes him to the Tennessee state prison system. In a written report, John Wright says that Eric Glover "does seem to show sincere remorse for his actions and for the death of Mrs. Lee."

Wright has interviewed Eric at prison in Tiptonville, Tennessee. However later, when Bob writes to Eric and asks for a meeting, he gets no reply.

Antonio has tried to commit suicide and is in solitary confinement during this time. He responds to a letter from Wright. In it he describes how he suspects a conspiracy in any attempt to get help for Mrs. Lee's husband in the case, or to provide any further information.

Wright has better luck when he interviews Inmate No. 298702, Robert Carpenter, at Turney Center Industrial Complex Prison in Hickman County near Nashville on April 23, 2003.

"I met with Robert and the interview lasted a little over two hours," the investigator reports later.

"When he arrived at the interview room he had what appeared to be six to eight letters inside envelopes with rubber bands around them."

Were the letters confessions from the other two? Did they contain new information that had never come out about the crime? Could Bob learn more about Ann's last hours?

Robert Carpenter says he'd like to turn over the letters and the information they contain, but he wants assurances they won't affect any future appeals on his behalf.

Wright describes Robert as "cautious and somewhat guarded" but reports that he seems to be ready to hand over the letters. As for any remorse for what he did: he showed none to Wright.

"The impression I got, " Wright wrote, "was that Robert Carpenter did what he felt he had to do at the time Mrs. Lee was murdered and it seems apparent to me that his judgment ... would be the same if presented with a similar situation in the future."

The question of whether Bob Lee would want to visit Robert at the prison and ask for the letters is left to him. Bob doesn't take long to think it over.

"I was ready to go. If he had helpful information, for my lawsuit or anything else, I was prepared to ask him in person."

It seems like Bob's last and best chance for a little more insight or to hear some utterance of regret.

That same month Bob charters a small plane. Lawyer Gary Smith accompanies him. They fly east for two hours in a heavy spring rainstorm. The Beechcraft King Air is rocked repeatedly but lands safely at a small airport near the prison. The private investigator meets them with a car.

"I'll never forget that day," Bob remembers many years later.

"I was very anxious. My heart rate could have been measured in hertz, it was beating so fast. I was going to be face-to-face with Ann's primary killer."

The three men are escorted to a small room with table and chairs above the prison pod where Robert Carpenter lives. They don't have long to wait.

Robert, looking well-groomed, walks in. Three tough-looking guards accompany him. Carpenter sits at the table, across from Bob. Two guards sit on either side of him and one takes a position at the end of the table.

Bob is thinking, "He doesn't look any worse for wear. He looks younger in fact than he did when he was on trial."

Carpenter looks around the room, sniffs and then nods across the table at Bob.

"How ya doin'?"

"I'm doing all right," Bob says, his voice uneven, higher pitched than usual.

Bob remembers later he wasn't feeling all that well. His heart was pounding and his tongue felt thick.

Attorney Smith points to the envelope Robert is holding and asks if he's going to give that to them.

"Maybe. Or maybe later."

Everyone looks at the prisoner expectantly. His face suddenly hardens and he has nothing more to say.

After a pause of a few seconds ("It seemed like hours to me," Bob says later), Robert stands and indicates to the guard he wants to leave. Everyone in the room gets up and they parade out of the room and down a hall to an elevator. The elevator door opens, Robert gives a half smile and hands the envelope to Smith, then steps inside. The door closes on Robert's face, his eyes on Bob.

Smith opens the envelope.

Inside are three blank sheets of paper.

Bob stares at the paper, feeling foolish. Smith calls the guard station and a guard asks Robert about the sheets. He has a mocking reply:

"The words must've fallen off."

144

That very day Bob abandons any hope that the men will repent of their crime or seek some kind of mercy from him. He doesn't feel the trip was a waste of time and effort, though.

For Bob Lee now absolutely knows that it is up to him — him alone — to finish a journey he never planned to take.

* * *

Now it is 20 years on.

Twenty years after the three young men were found guilty of state and federal counts of first degree murder, among other felony charges. They are held in two Tennessee prisons under what the state Department of Corrections calls minimum-level security. They dress daily in prison blues.

Robert Carpenter has a round face now and a slim mustache. He remains at the five feet five inches of height that he was when arrested. Prisoner number 298702 now lives inside the Morgan County Correctional Complex in east Tennessee.

Carpenter's brother Antonio Carpenter, prisoner number 308289, is incarcerated at the Hardeman County Correctional Facility in Whiteville, Tennessee, not far from where he was arrested. He has reached a height of six feet two inches and weighs 165 pounds. His head is shaved. He otherwise looks much the same as when he was on trial.

Eric Glover, prisoner number 317432, remains behind bars at the same facility where Antonio is imprisoned. Glover now is stocky and sports a trim goatee.

None of the three ever has agreed to tell exactly what happened in the woods a mile off Yager Road. Nevertheless, the Carpenters will spend their lives behind prison bars. Glover may

This is the site of the Carpenter place two decades after Ann's murder. Trees and underbrush flourish where the house once stood.

come up for parole one day almost three decades away. All three men already have lived longer in prison than they lived free.

* * *

Twenty years on, life proceeds apace on the busy Collierville highway where people periodically pull into Slot 22 at the Sonic and call in their orders. Young workers hustle in and out with their trays of food.

Car windows roll down and money and food are quickly exchanged.

Twenty years on, Ricky Wilson drives and remembers a day he'll never forget. He has agreed to drive the route he took in pursuit of the trio that hot summer day. It's the first time he's done so, recreating the most memorable case of his law enforcement career. Detective Chuck Pugh was his mentor then. Now Wilson tries to be that to young officers for whom the Ann Lee murder and the subsequent 22-mile chase is a story from yesterday ... but one they like to hear recounted.

As his Fayette County Sheriff's Department SUV takes the curves through rural Fayette County and then into Mississippi, he relates every moment of that pursuit in rich detail. He pauses only once, to get out and nudge a mean-looking snapping turtle across the highway to safety. Then he resumes his drive, recounting the chase all along the route.

He easily finds the narrow strip of land where he and others chased Ann Lee's vehicle off U.S. 72 and into a wheat farm.

"Here's where I crossed over the median and tried to head them off. Look — my gosh! This is exactly where we went careening into the field. I can remember it all perfectly. See where those trees are that mark that sudden turn toward the east? That's where I almost ended up in the steep gully."

Twenty years on Bob Lee slows his own vehicle on Yager Road. He too is reliving that day from the perspective of a husband hearing the worst news possible. He is looking for the gravel and dirt drive into the Carpenter place.

"It's got to be along here some where's," he says, driving slowly. Bob no longer is the vengeful widower who yearns to kill the killers. He has learned to control such feelings, to empty his heart of hate. He spends more time now in appreciation of his family and his life and, yes, life's fragility.

There is little traffic on this Saturday morning. He pulls to a stop. On the other side of the road is an old cemetery bordered by shrubs where Detective Pugh parked his cruiser that afternoon, waiting in case the green Blazer came into view. There's little to see now of the spot where Robert Carpenter turned onto the road And the pursuit began.

The house is gone. The driveway is barely perceptible to the eye. Hip-high weeds and trees approaching 20 years old hide any sign of the house. The old dirt road that led to the lonely killing spot is barely discernable. It seems fitting that nature has reclaimed her ground here for this isn't where the best memories are kept.

A much better place is the Germantown, Tennessee, civic park that is the home of the Germantown Charity Horse Show.[v] There on a small bit of lawn in the shade of a crepe myrtle stands a permanent stone monument to Ann. On the stone's face is a three-dimensional sculpture created by her daughter Liz. It depicts

The face of the monument at Germantown Civic Park includes a sculpture by daughter Liz and poem by son Robert, Jr.

equestrian teacher Ann with a horse, a young rider in training, and loyal dog Otis.

Next to this image is a poem written by Ann's son Robert Lee, Jr. It is entitled "Remember me."

Remember Me

By Robert Lee Jr.

To the living, I am gone
To the sorrowful, I will never return
To the angry, I was cheated

But to the happy, I am at peace
And to the faithful, I have never left

I cannot speak, but I can listen
I cannot be seen, but I can be heard

149

At Road's End

To my devoted dog Otis,
I will always be by your side
As you were by mine

So,
As you stand upon a shore
Gazing at a beautiful sea –
Remember me

Remember me in your heart,
Your thoughts and your memories
Of the times we cried,
The times we fought,
The times we laughed

For if you always think of me,
I will never be gone from your side.

EPILOGUE

It is a fine cloudless day in spring.

Bob Lee, a man on a long journey, is on a short stroll today. He's walking a Schnauzer through his snug Collierville neighborhood of stately houses, trees and shrubs. The canine, ever alert, spots one of the rabbits that also live in the neighborhood and sprints off to the end of her leash.

"Sophie! Come here, girl." Sophie is the mirror image of another beloved dog named Otis. She's quick to the hunt of a hare.

"C'mon, now."

Soon she's back at his side.

Barbara Ann Lee — wife, mother, horsewoman with countless friends and acquaintances — enjoyed life and shared her joy with many. Faithful Otis was her steady companion, but he lost her one afternoon in the shadow of woods, in the shadow of murder.

She was only 63 years old.

Her life ended ferociously, mindlessly at the hands of three young men who cared nothing about her or what she stood for. Two of the men now will never live outside prison walls. A third only will be eligible to enter the outer world when he is older than Ann was when she died.

Ann's arbitrary and needless death marked the start of a difficult sojourn of the soul for Bob.

This proved a winding trail, one leading ultimately toward forgiveness. A treacherous walk that took 20 years of time and uncountable detours, dead ends and deep potholes to endure. His has been a journey requiring help from friends and strangers, family members and counselors, lawyers and prosecutors and

**Bob Lee and his dog Sophie enjoy the late-winter sun after a walk,
21 years after Ann Lee's murder.**

news reporters. One that included a rediscovered faith in God and in other people.

Most of all, it has been a learning experience, and one that Bob likes to share. He enjoys the possibility of helping others on their difficult treks. He also strives daily to preserve his hard-fought perspective as time goes by.

For forgiveness, one must see, is a muscle that needs to be

exercised. It is a practice that requires recitation and repetition.

What did Bob learn about this act of forgiving?

He first learned what it is not.

Forgiving isn't the same thing as achieving justice or the "righting of un-rightable wrongs."

It is not acceptance of another's wrongful deed or immoral act. It is not acquiescence to formidable forces or requirements pushed by others. And it is not forgetting.

No, it's none of those things. It is something deeper still.

Forgiveness, Bob will tell you, is a total change of heart and a surrender to God's edict that "vengeance is mine." It is a release of internal anger and hate and wish for revenge.

It is the metaphorical dropping of a hot coal before it burns through one's very being.

It is a never-ending movement toward the light. The light of one's own heart and mind. Light just like the shining of this sunny morning, itself like many fine mornings and simple walks with a pal named Sophie.

Forgiving, Bob knows now, is being sure that when the work is done, light and life will overcome the worst of the shadows.

THE END

ENDNOTES

[i] According to HorseProperties.net, Shelby County, Tennessee has more horses per capita than any other county in the nation. 3.2 million of the state's 10 million farm acres are devoted to the horse industry.

[ii] Susan Gillpatrick, Med, LPC, CTS. Susan today has more than 20 years experience in crisis management and behavioral health, and specializes in leading a variety of comprehensive crisis prevention and response programs, as well as personal and professional growth training. She is a Licensed Professional Counselor and Mental Health Service Provider, a Board-Certified Expert in Traumatic Stress by the American Academy of Experts in Traumatic Stress, a Certified Trauma Specialist by the Association of Traumatic Stress Specialist, and a Certified Employee Assistance Professional.

[iii] Federal executions came to a halt in 2003 as questions arose over the use of drugs and their effects. The hiatus lasted until July 2019 when U.S. Attorney General William Barr announced executions would resume. Ten people were put to death by federal officials in 2020 according to the national Death Penalty Information Center.

[iv] In March 2018 in Nashville Bob was awarded the Governor's Volunteer Star certificate "for outstanding community service in the highest traditions of the State of Tennessee (Volunteer State)."

[v] The Germantown Charity Horse Show celebrated its 72nd anniversary in 2020. It is one of several major horse shows in the

U.S. governed by the U.S. Equestrian Federation. The Germantown show includes hunters, jumpers, Arabians, American Saddlebred and Tennessee Walking horse. Ann Lee managed the West Tennessee Hunter Jumper Show there.